A SHORT ACCOUNT OF THE LACCADIVE ISLANDS AND MINICOY

A SHORT ACCOUNT
OF THE
LACCADIVE ISLANDS AND MINICOY

R. H. ELLIS

GYAN

Published by

GYAN

Gyan Publishing House
5, Ansari Road
Daryaganj, New Delhi-110002
Phone: 011-47034999, 9811692060
E-mail: books@gyanbooks.com

Distribution Network
gyanbooks.com
India, USA, Canada, UK, Australia, France

ISBN : 978-81-212-4007-9 (PB)
First Published, Madras, 1924

2nd Impression 2020

Printed at: Gyan Press, Delhi.

A Short Account of the Laccadive Islands and Minicoy
Author: R. H. Ellis

A SHORT ACCOUNT

OF THE

LACCADIVE ISLANDS AND MINICOY

BY

R. H. ELLIS, I.C.S.

MADRAS
PRINTED BY THE SUPERINTENDENT, GOVERNMENT PRESS

1924

NOTE

References to records have been given wherever possible. Much of the contents of Chapters IV, V and VI is the result of personal observation and enquiry. Sir W. Robinson's report of his visit to the South Kanara Islands in 1845 is throughout referred to as Robinson I, and his report upon the Malabar Islands in 1847 as Robinson II.

R.H

CONTENTS.

CHAPTER I.

PHYSICAL DESCRIPTION.

CHAPTER II.

HISTORY.

CHAPTER III.

ADMINISTRATION AND REVENUE.

CHAPTER IV.

THE PEOPLE.

CHAPTER V.

OCCUPATIONS AND TRADE.

CHAPTER VI.

GAZETTEER.

APPENDICES.

MAPS.

A SHORT ACCOUNT OF THE LACCADIVE ISLANDS AND MINICOY.

CHAPTER I.

PHYSICAL DESCRIPTION.

THE Laccadive Archipelago forms with the Maldives a long narrow belt extending due north and south from the level of the South Kanara district in lat. 14° N., to Addu atoll in lat. 0° 40′ S. The Laccadives extend down to lat. 10° N., and consist of a series of isolated islands and submerged banks, mostly of small size. The Maldives commence in lat. 7°10′ N. and form a sequence of large submerged banks and islands. Intermediate between the two groups lies Minicoy in lat. 8° 20′ N., 114 miles distant from Kalpeni and 71 miles from Thavandifobe the nearest Maldive. The two groups are situated on a common bank which nowhere, so far as is known, lies at a greater depth than 1,200 fathoms. Soundings have been obtained of 1,195 fathoms in the Nine Degree channel, north of Minicoy, and of 1,179 in the Eight Degree channel south of that island. The 1,000-fathom line has been traced everywhere between the Laccadives and India and there is no trace of any connection by shoals with the mainland. The 2,000-fathom line runs across from Ceylon to the Maldives, turns southwards along their eastern face at a distance of not more than 30 or 40 miles, bends north round their southern extremity and extends up on the west even closer to them than on the east, becoming somewhat more distant where it reaches the Laccadives. At Minicoy it is about 100 miles distant. **GENERAL FEATURES.**

Excluding Minicoy, which cannot be said to belong to one group more than the other, the Laccadive group consists of seventeen banks, Elikalpeni, Androth, Kalpeni and Suheli being outliers separated by over 1,100 fathoms, while the rest are included within a common 956-fathom line. Of the seventeen, Valiyapani or Munzal 71 miles by 14 miles, Sesostris 15 miles by 8 miles, Coradive 20 miles by 5½ miles, and Elikalpeni, are submerged banks without a definite encircling reef. Androth is situated at the south of a bank 11½ miles long, east and west, by 6 miles broad. Ameni and Pitti are at opposite ends of a bank 26 miles long. Both these banks still show traces of the typical "Atoll"* shape. Agathi bank has two atolls, Agathi itself, united by a bank at a depth of 7 to 10 fathoms with a northern atoll containing three islets, Bangaram, Tinnakara and Parli. The remainder Bitra, Kiltan, Chetlat, Kavarathi, Kalpeni, Cheriyapani, Byramgore, Peremul, Kadamat and Suheli are perfect single ring-reefs. Byramgore and Peremul are submerged. Cheriyapani has sand banks on its north and east sides. The others have islands along the inner side of the eastern arc of the reef, are planted up with coconuts, and with the exception of Suheli and Bitra are inhabited.

METEOROLOGICAL. Winds. The winds experienced are those of the two monsoons, influenced by the proximity of the Indian coast. The north-east monsoon becomes established about the end of November and continues until March. During this period the prevailing winds are northerly, with long calms, and but little or no heavy weather. Often, however, the wind blows strongly for days at a time, especially among the northern islands, from the east or north-east.

The south-west monsoon usually becomes definitely set towards the end of May and continues regularly until September.

Storms. During the months intervening between the two monsoons, cyclonic storms or hurricanes are liable to occur. Hurricanes are said to visit the islands at intervals of about twelve years. As their centres usually lie well to the north they are little felt at Minicoy. The northern islands, however, have suffered severely. The most disastrous storm on record is that which burst upon the islands on 15th April 1847. It reached Kalpeni at about 8 p.m. from the east-north-east and seems to have moved in a west-north-west direction between the islands and the mainland. The line of islands nearest the coast suffered severely, while those further out were but little affected and the storm does not seem to have been felt at Minicoy at all. Its destructive effects were aggravated by its having occurred at the season of spring tides, and by its having broken upon the eastern unprotected side of the islands. The storm reached Androth between 12 p.m. and 2 a.m. on the morning of April 16th and burst upon Kiltan about an hour after sunrise. Another storm visited Kavarathi on 5th

Robinson II, p. 156.

* The term "Atoll" is derived from a Mahl word *Atolu* signifying an administrative division. There are thirteen of these in the Maldives, many of them consisting of a single island each. Hence the transferred meaning—vide Gardiner, p. 155.

November 1891 and did considerable damage. It seems to have been purely a local disturbance and was scarcely felt on the neighbouring islands. It necessitated large remissions and reductions in the cowle rents on Kavarathi.

Currents are extremely variable. During the north-east monsoon, a strong current sets to the northward between the islands and the mainland at the rate of 25 to 35 miles per 24 hours, and in the south-west monsoon a similar southerly current prevails. Currents.

At Minicoy there is a rise of 5 feet 9 inches at spring tides and 3 feet 6 inches at neaps. The tides in the more northern islands are probably higher. Tides.

The rainfall on the islands decreases from south to north. There are three rain guages, at Minicoy, Kalpeni and Ameni. On Minicoy the rainfall is about 100 inches, while on Kalpeni it is only between 60 and 65 inches in the year, and on Ameni it is just below 60. In the Maldives it is said to reach 150 inches. Rainfall.

The greater part of the rain falls during the south-west monsoon in the months of June and July. During the rest of the year, except in November and December when the north-east monsoon brings heavy showers, there is but little rain. The highest recorded rainfall at Ameni for 24 hours has been 10 inches.

The temperature in the shade varies between 70° and 90° F. Agathi is the hottest of the inhabited islands, and the neighbouring islets, Bangaram, Tinnakara and Parli, strike the visitor as unbearable. To avoid the heat at night on Agathi the people erect small cadjan " sleeping boxes " on the beach. Temperature.

The submerged banks rise almost precipitously from the common bank upon which the group stands. Soundings seem to show a sheer drop from about 25 fathoms to 400 or 500 fathoms or even more. GEOLOGY.

Round the typical ring-reefs the drop is less abrupt. The ring is formed by a "reef-flat" 50 or even 150 yards wide, almost level, covered with small boulders of coral limestone, and usually submerged a few feet under water. At Kalpeni, Kadamat, Androth, Chetlat and Kiltan, however, the reef-flat is well exposed at low tide. Often the reef-flat is quite bare on the seaward side and the boulders are collected in a regular zone about 30 yards wide, on the lagoon side. The reef-flat ends abruptly on the lagoon side with a drop of 3 or 4 feet, but the rock has been found to extend under the sand of the lagoon bed to the reef-flat on the opposite side. On the seaward side, what is termed a reef-platform slopes gradually, often in a series of terraces, from the reef-flat until a depth of 20 fathoms is reached. Here a precipitous drop commences. Soundings increase suddenly, within perhaps not more than a ship's length, to 160 or 200 fathoms. This precipice lies on an average only 400 or 500 yards from the reef-flat and it is easy to see how dangerous the islands are to approach and what difficult anchorages they afford. There are in fact only one or two places on each reef where a ship can safely anchor and even at these it is no unusual occurrence for the anchor to slip off a terrace in 6 fathoms into perhaps 20 fathoms. From a depth of about 200 fathoms the bottom slopes very much more gradually until the level of the common bank is reached.

The slope from the reef flat is always much more abrupt on the eastern than on the western side of the atolls and the precipitous drop lies very much closer in. In fact in some islands there is no marked reef-platform at all on the eastern face and the slope commences from the edge of the reef-flat itself. This is the case at Chetlat, Kalpeni and Kadamat where the 100-fathom line is not 150 yards from the shore. Except at Kadamat, the exposed portion of the reef-flat in this position is usually very narrow, but it can always be traced along the sea beach, appearing from under the sand or boulders that form the beach and sloping gently under the water. At Kadamat the reef-flat extends 150 yards or so from the beach and is completely exposed at low tide.

At Chetlat, Kiltan, Kavarathi and Agathi, the reef-rock can be traced into the lagoon round both ends of the island proper, as an outcrop from under the sand, corresponding in width with the reef-flat round the western arc of the atoll. The outcrop ends in a "cliff" 4 or 5 feet above the level of the western reef-flat. The cliff is due to the sand and boulders of the island proper, which have protected the rock beneath from the eroding action of the sea. In the other islands no cliff or outcrop, if one exists, is exposed and the sand of the lagoon beach is continuous with the sand of the sea beach on the northern and southern faces. Everywhere the rock forming the reef-flat is a coral conglomerate. Blastings at Kalpeni and Minicoy showed this very clearly.

The lagoon is a shallow saucer-shaped depression. Its depth is not usually more than two or three fathoms on the Laccadives although on the Maldives an average of 20 or 30 fathoms is common. The southern end of the lagoon is sometimes much silted up. At Kalpeni, the southern part of the big lagoon is quite dry at low water for almost half a mile from the shore, while at Minicoy the depth of water at low tide is only a few inches. In the deeper water great bosses and beds of coral grow up from the bottom to within a foot or two of the surface with a luxuriance unknown on most coral islands, where coral growths inside the lagoon are usually very rare. Seen through a water-glass these masses of coral appear a veritable wonderland of beauty, with fishes of marvellous colouring darting in and out of their fairy grottoes. It appears to be probable that all the lagoons will in the course of time fill up through the combined action of the sea in depositing sand and of the shallow-water corals.

The island proper is usually a narrow bank of sand piled up by the action of sea and wind against the inner side of the eastern arc of the atoll, two or three or even five miles in length, and varying in breadth from half a mile to a few yards. On all the islands the sand is increasing steadily, but at varying rates, on the lagoon side, and the islands are in consequence growing. The growth is particularly marked at Kiltan where the cutcherry was once on the edge of the beach. Several feet under the sand on all the islands except Minicoy and Kalpeni lies a horizontal bed of coral limestone a few inches or perhaps two feet and more in depth. It appears to be continuous with the conglomerate of the reef. There is no indication that any similar bed of limestone is now in process of formation in any position and it may perhaps be that the limestone bed indicates a previous sea bottom at a depth beyond the action of the waves. The stone is much used for building and to its presence is attributed the supply of good water which can be obtained everywhere if a well is bored through the limestone bed. Similar limestone (beach sandstone) is found on the lagoon beaches of most of the islands, but the bed, instead of being horizontal, appears to dip towards the lagoon at the same angle as the lagoon beach. The beach sandstone is quarried by the people for building purposes. It reforms after about two years in some positions.

On the sea face, the land is fringed on all the islands except Agathi, Ameni and Kadamath, by a more or less marked ridge of coral debris and coral rock. This ridge attains a height of nearly 20 feet at places on Minicoy. At the north end of Kalpeni it is formed by huge boulders (Negro-heads) of much weathered coral. It is known to have been the result of the great storm of 1847 and probably other big storms have added to it.

Two theories have been put forward to account for the formation of coral islands, both based upon the now well-attested fact that reef-building corals only grow between a depth of about 30 fathoms and the surface. One is the well-known Darwinian theory, one of the most brilliant examples of an explanation for natural phenomena arrived at by pure reason, no direct evidence in support of it having yet been discovered. Darwin assumed that the corals commenced their growth at a suitable level, round some peak or volcanic crater. If, then, the land commenced to subside so slowly that the corals could maintain their position at the right level for growth, the reef would grow upwards, while the crater, if it was ever exposed above the surface of the sea, would disappear and become covered with corals, which, however, would grow much less rapidly than the better nourished corals on the exterior of the reef, thus forming the central lagoon. The outer corals would grow till they reached their limit at the surface and would form the circular reef so typical of coral islands.

The other theory postulates a submerged bank at a suitable depth, i.e., something less than 30 fathoms, upon which the corals can grow. Subsidence of the land is not, as in the first theory, assumed, and if the coral bank is to increase laterally it can only be by the outgrowth of the reef corals upon the accumulated debris from the reef, which the action of the sea tends to pile up round the base of the original bank and which the coral growths then consolidate. The slopes off the Laccadive reefs are everywhere so precipitous that, upon this theory, so far as they are concerned, it must only be supposed that there has been no lateral widening and that the corals have grown almost straight up to the surface.

Professor Stanley Gardiner, as the Balfour student of Cambridge University for 1899–1900, examined minutely the geology of the Maldives and Minicoy in those years, and his report (in the "Fauna Flora and Geography of the Maldives and Laccadives") throws some interesting light upon the formation of these reefs. His investigation of the Maldives leads him to reject the Darwinian theory as an adequate explanation of the manner in which they were formed. As he points out, both archipelagoes are so similarly situated and so closely connected that both have probably been formed in the same way, and thus probably Darwin's theory does not apply to the Laccadives either.

The grounds upon which Professor Gardiner bases his opinion may be briefly summarised. With the exception of Addu and Suădiva, which are typical atolls like the Laccadive atolls, the remainder of the Maldives form a well defined line of banks, 325 miles in length without any breaks between them of really considerable extent. This line is single at each end but doubles at the centre, where it encloses a long narrow strip of water between its two series of shoals. Soundings show that the banks arise as so many plateaux from a common plateau which has a general depth of about 200 fathoms. The banks reach the surface in every variety of form. The smaller ones are perfect atolls. The larger are irregularly elliptical rings composed of separate reefs, and these reefs in their turn may be either mere reefs or almost perfect atolls with lagoons. Inside these irregular rings, again, are dotted more or less numerous reefs or tiny atolls. There is no sign that the present irregular rings ever formed a continuous ring reef. The fact that the passages between their component reefs are as deep or deeper than the interior of the bank seems almost conclusive on the point. Each component reef appears to be a separate entity which has grown up and developed by itself, influenced, of course, by its position and by the reefs in its vicinity, but never directly connected with them. Moreover the floor of the lagoon is almost perfectly level and does not shelve gradually to the centre as it would do if Darwin's theory were correct.

Obviously a formation of this kind is not satisfactorily explained by the Darwinian theory. The fact that miniature atolls are found inside the irregular rings seems to preclude the supposition that the rings evidence the subsidence of any land at their centres. The flatness of the lagoon bed seems a fatal objection to the theory. Professor Gardiner's own view is that the reefs and atolls have been formed by the upgrowth of corals from a common plateau. The occurrence among the Laccadives of the submerged banks with no trace of the atoll formation, of such formations as Androth, an atoll upon a much larger bank, and Ameni and Pitti, two atolls at each end of a long bank add very great support to his view.

If this conclusion is correct, the islands are formations of coral built up from underlying banks or plateaux which the reef-building corals found at a depth favourable to their existence. How the banks themselves came to be formed must remain matter for conjecture. Perhaps they represent portions of that old continent which is supposed to have existed in the Jurassic and Cretaceous ages between India and Southern and Central Africa and which, it is supposed, was broken up by the mighty changes in early tertiary times to which also the upheaval of the Himalayas was due.

But, as Professor Gardiner has pointed out, the present conformation of the islands is due to something more than the mere upgrowth of corals. The conglomerate found along the eastern sea-face of all the islands is positive evidence of upheaval or at least of alteration in sea level. It is obvious that it could never have formed in its present position, exposed to the direct action of the sea. Its erosion by the sea is in fact at the present moment going steadily on. Professor Gardiner suggests an upheaval of at least 24 feet. In calculating this, he assumes that the ridge of coral boulders above the conglomerate represents the results of aerial denudation upon the conglomerate exposed above the sea by the upheaval. It is, however, permissible to point out that this ridge is known to have been thrown up on some of the Laccadives by the great storm of 1847. The ridges on these islands differ in no way from those on the other islands, and the observer would certainly never suspect from their appearance that these ridges were anything but what are commonly known as storm beaches. Professor Gardiner also assumes that the conglomerate commences from the level of the reef-flat, which he takes to be the upper face of the reef. It is unfortunate that he made no borings into the reef-flat, for recent blastings at Kalpeni and Minicoy show that the surface of the reef-flat there is also conglomerate. Extensive borings on coral islands in the Pacific have shown a coral conglomerate down to a depth of over 1,000 feet and the fact appears to be that the kind of rock produced by the reef-building corals is a coral conglomerate. Moreover, the level surface of the reef-flat has probably been caused by the erosive action of the sea which always tends to produce a level bottom. It probably therefore marks the lowest limit of erosion not the highest limit of the upward growth of the reef building corals. It follows that there is no possibility of calculating, even approximately, the amount of the upheaval though the conjecture that the limestone bed represents the previous sea bottom would set a maximum upwards for it.

The difference in level between the top of the conglomerate on the eastern arc and the level of the reef-flat on the western arc of the atolls would be due to the greater violence of the seas during the monsoon upon the western arc, and to the protective influence of the sand and boulders piled up against and upon the eastern arc. But difficulties present themselves as to the original position of the living reef and as to the manner of the formation of the conglomerate and of the lagoon, which are at present impossible of complete solution. Recent investigation in America seems to show that the atoll form is due to the action of the prevailing wind and currents upon an originally more or less straight bank, the wind and currents curving the growing ends round till they meet in a circle. The lagoon, it is thought, is due to the growth of the corals at the centre having been greatly retarded by deposits of sand and silt from the sea.

The only definite conclusion that has been arrived at, then, is that the islands are not as one might think, atolls in process of formation, but the remains of originally more or less perfect atolls, exposed to marine and aerial denudation either by upheaval or by an alteration in sea level. Actual upheaval is perhaps more probable than an alteration in the sea level and perhaps occurred about the same time that the Malabar Coast below the Ghats was raised above the sea. After the reefs were cut down to their present level, the "island" of sand has been piled up inside the lagoon by the wind and waves. The reefs must not, however, be regarded as "dead." A second period of growth is now taking place upon the reef platforms through the activity of the living corals which are slowly building up a fresh coral conglomerate in these positions. Some growth is also taking place in the lagoons.

The only other matter of any geological interest connected with the islands is the occurrence of small pieces of pumice which are to be found marking the lines of previous flood levels along the lagoon beaches of most of the islands. The source of the pumice was for long a mystery and it was attributed to the eruptions of some submarine volcano. Professor Gardiner, however, reported from enquiries among the people that pumice was unknown on the Maldives until about 1883, and suggested that it was the result of the eruption of Krakatoa in that year. This conjecture is borne out by the fact that on the Laccadives, in the years just subsequent to 1883, large beds of pumice were reported, which have now entirely disappeared. Only scattered pieces, much water-worn, are now found.

A full list of plants found on the islands is given at pages 1053—1055 of Professor Gardiner's "Fauna and Geography of the Maldives." Among trees the coconut is the commonest, the islands being covered with plantations. There are a few bread fruit trees, banyans, and tamarinds, on all the islands. The *puvarasu* (Thespesia populnea), the *punna* (Calophyllum inophyllum), the wild almond (Terminalia catappa) and the horse radish tree (Moringa pterygosperma) are fairly common. A species of tree cotton (*paruthi mara*) is found on Kalpeni and Androth and some true cotton grows wild on Bangaram ; the cotton obtained from both is used for making wicks for the lamps in the mosques. The Morinda citrifolia the root of which was once much used for dyeing, is found on Kalpeni and Androth. Limes were formerly cultivated very BOTANY.

largely in Ameni and Kavarathi and the export of pickled limes from these islands was considerable, but the trees have now nearly all died out owing to some pest. Fringing the beach in the uninhabited portions of every island are dense thickets of *chonam*, a small fragrant shrub from which a sort of tea is made, *cheruthalam* (Pemphis acidula) a bushy shrub which is cut for firewood and exported, *kanni* (Scævola Kœnigii) which also grows inland in great clumps rather like a rhododendron, and the wild heliotrope (Tournefolia argentea). The *kēyam* is a small tree found on the South Kanara Islands and Kavarathi from the wood of which the tholepin of the oar is made. The *patti* (Maceronga Roxburghii) is used for making rafts. The screw pine (Pandanus odoratissimus) grows everywhere and with a luxuriance unknown on the mainland: on the uninhabited islands the screw pine growth is from 20 to 30 feet high. Ferns are found in great quantities in the tottam at Androth, and mosses and lichens at Minicoy during the monsoon. The creeping purple convolvulus (Ipomœa biloba) is common everywhere. The red ixora (I. coccinea) is not uncommon, and in the tottam at Androth a white balsam occurs. On Minicoy and on the uninhabited islands the *ittala* (Dioscorea oppositifolia) is found. Its white tubers grow to a large size and are made into a kind of tapioca.

In the tottams on several of the islands a little coarse paddy, ragi, varagu, cholam, beans and sweet potatoes are grown, while round their houses the people cultivate patches of *chēmbu*, a kind of yam.

ZOOLOGY. It is impossible here to give the very technical information that is required for the identification of the fishes, crabs and lower organisms. Full particulars will be found in Professor Gardiner's book, where his collections have been catalogued and described minutely.

Cowries of all kinds from the small money cowry to the large handsome spotted varieties, giant clams (Tridacna) and huge specimens of the giant pinna are common on all the reefs. Holothurians or sea slugs of three varieties are found in the lagoons. An edible octopus (*Appalū*) is found on the reefs, which is caught at night with the aid of flares.

Hermit crabs (Coenobita) abound. Almost every suitable dead shell on the beach will be found occupied by one, and as the visitor strolls along the beach he will be surprised at first to find these seemingly dead shells coming to life and rolling out of his way. A big dark red variety is found inland which has sometimes been known to occupy a small coconut shell in the absence of any shell of suitable size. Ocypod crabs, greyish in colour, with the eyes placed at the end of short stalks, are also very common. They are caught for food. On the uninhabited islands they grow to a comparatively large size and the sand excavated from their burrows gives the beach an extraordinary appearance, rather as if countless pails of sand had been emptied at irregular intervals all over the beach. Grapsoid crabs, barred green and brown, will be found crawling over every rock.

A remarkable feature of the Laccadive marine fauna is its similarity to the marine fauna of the Atlantic in the region of the West Indies. Two of the most remarkable Laccadive Crustaceans the large Isopod (Bathynomus giganteus) the blind spiny lobster (Phoberus caecus) and the spiny hermit crab (Lithodes Agassizii) are found in the Carribean Sea and one of the commonest Laccadive sea urchins (Palæopneustes Hemingi) is very doubtfully distinct from P. cristatus found off the West Indies. There are also many corals and fish common to both regions.

Fish are abundant. Many of the small kinds found in the lagoons are wonderfully coloured. Among common kinds are Surgeon fish (Naseus) with two or four knife-edged spines near the tail with which they can inflict a dangerous and sometimes even a fatal wound: gar fish, long narrow fish which have the upper jaw prolonged into a long sharp beak; spiny sun-fish which as a protection can blow themselves out to a relatively enormous size; the extraordinary box fish whose skin has become so ossified that it can only move its fins, tail, and eyes; and the *palli* which has four enormous teeth capable of biting a finger clean off. Sharks and sword-fish are frequently caught, and shark fins when dried are exported to Malabar and Colombo. The bonito appears to be found in the deep sea off all the islands but is only fished for on Minicoy. Flying fish are common everywhere. Skates, sometimes of enormous size, measuring 12 feet or more from fin to fin, are common in the lagoons. They are caught, generally by harpooning, in the months of July and August; they are found in the greatest numbers in the waters off Androth and Kalpeni. In a good season three or four hundred of these huge fish are secured. The fish is cut into slices and cured by being dried in the sun or smoked over a fire. The dried slices roasted and pounded up with coconut are regarded as a great delicacy.

Two kinds of turtle are found, the Green Turtle and the Hawksbill. The Green Turtle is killed for its fat which yields a very valuable oil. It is caught at night with nets when it comes into the shoal water to feed. When the turtles are located, a net is run hastily out between them and the deep water and they are chased into it and caught. Turtles are also easily caught in the day time from a boat. When chased by a boat, although at first they can swim away for short distances at a great speed, they very soon tire and are easily caught by the boatmen, who jump overboard on top of them. The female turtle comes up at night to the sand above high-water mark and there lays her eggs, from 100 to 200 in number, in a neat little pile, at one spot in a big excavation which she digs in the sand, 15 or 20 feet long and 3 to 5 feet deep. The eggs have a white parchment-like shell and are the size and shape of a ping-pong ball. The young turtles all hatch out at much the same time and immediately make for the sea. Alcock ("A Naturalist in Indian Seas," page 85) gives an interesting account of a hatch which he witnessed: "There was a tremendous commotion in the dry sand and out of it there emerged a swarm of little objects looking like beetles, which all with one consent made for the sea. Even when we caught them and started them off in the opposite direction some unerring instinct caused them at once to turn round towards the sea again."

The Hawksbill Turtle which is less common and does not grow to such a size as the Green Turtle, produces the tortoise shell of commerce.

BIRDS.

(i) *Permanent residents*—

Puffinus persicus.

Buttorides Javanica. The little Green Heron.

Ardea cinerea. The Common Heron. These birds breed at Minicoy on Viringilli.

Nettium crecca. The Common Teal.

Gallinula phœnicula. The white breasted water hen.

Dromas ardeola. The Crab Plover.

Sterna fuliginosa. The Sooty Tern.

Sterna melanauchen. The Black Naped Tern.

Sterna bernsteini.

Eudynamis sonorata. The Koel. Breeds on Kavarathi where there is a large colony of these birds.

Corvus splendens. The Crow. Found only on Ameni, Androth and Kalpeni. It is said that a saint prohibited them from ever coming to any of the other islands because one once defiled his head. Five or six have now (1922) appeared on Minicoy.

(ii) *Regular visitors*—

Charadrius fulvus. The Golden Plover.

Totanus hypoleucus. The Common Sandpiper.

Numenius phæops. The Whimbrel.
Falco tinnunculus. The Kestrel.
Circus macrurus. The Pole Harrier.
Circus cineraceus. Montagu's Harrier.
Hirundo urbica. The Martin.

Pitti, a mere sand bank with no trees or vegetation, is the breeding ground for thousands of sea birds and at that season of the year is regularly visited by the islanders in search of eggs.

Major Alcock, I.M.S., in "A Naturalist in Indian Seas," gives an interesting description of the scene upon Pitti during the breeding season. He writes: "From the ship it looked like a barren sand bank and nothing more, but as our landing party drew near, the boat suddenly became enveloped in a dense crowd of shrieking sea birds. On landing we found every foot of the ground above high-water mark literally carpeted with young terns of two species, many living and nearly full fledged, many dead and rotting, and many reduced to clean picked skeletons with only the quill feathers still sticking to the wing-bones. There were no traces of nests or of any materials out of which nests could have been made, so that the parent birds must have laid and hatched their eggs on the bare sand. We soon discovered that one great cause of the wholesale destruction of young birds was the voracity of swarms of large hermit crabs (Cœnobita), for again and again we found recently killed birds, in all the beauty of their first speckled plumage, being torn to pieces by a writhing pack of these ghastly crustaceans."

Bitra, also, when Sir W. Robinson visited it in 1845, was the breeding ground of enormous numbers of sea birds, but none have been known to breed there in more recent times. Robinson I, p. 26.

MAMMALS.

Except Whales, and porpoises, there are no Mammals that can be properly called indigenous, and, excluding domesticated animals, only two species are found on the islands at all, the common Musk Shrew of India (Crocidura murina) and the ubiquitous rat. The latter has become to a considerable extent arboreal in habit and does incalculable damage by boring into and eating the green nuts of the coconut. There appear to be two different varieties, a large reddish rat (Mus rattus rufinus) found only on Androth, Agathi, Kavarathi and Kalpeni, and a smaller dark brown rat (Mus rattus Alexandrinus) found on the other islands. Both varieties are common throughout the whole of India. It is strange that they should have colonised separate islands.

Whales, probably of the bottle nose variety, are frequently washed ashore dead, while porpoises sometimes venture quite close to the islands and are at once pursued by the islanders who seek to drive them into shallow water and so to capture them.

NOTE.—Bibliography for Chap. I:—

Prof. Stanley Gardiner: Fauna, Flora and Geography of the Maldives and Laccadives.

Major Alcock, I.M.S.: A naturalist in Indian Seas.

The Malabar District Manual.

CHAPTER II.

HISTORY.

Universal local tradition points to the period of anarchy and confusion on the coast which followed the era of Cheraman Perumāl as the time when the islands were first occupied. One tradition asserts that the earliest settlers were the ship-wrecked members of an expedition that set out from Malabar in quest of the Perumāl, who was believed to have gone to Mecca. Whether there is any foundation in fact for this or not, there must obviously have been also a very considerable voluntary immigration, especially of the lower classes, from the coast. The islands supposed to have been peopled first are Ameni, Kalpeni, Androth, Kavarathi and Agathi. The upper classes of the first four of these islands still claim to trace their descent from Nayar or even Nambudiri families on the mainland, and these islands are known in consequence as "tarawad" islands in distinction to the other, or Melacheri, islands. That the claim is not unfounded is shown by many of the house-names (e.g., Valiya illam, Kākā illam). The lower castes, chiefly Tiyyars and Mukkuvars, from whom the Melacheri class is descended, settled on the larger islands as servants of the better classes, and also populated exclusively Agathi and the smaller islands. Kiltan, Chetlat and Kadamat appear to have been occupied only recently, for Lieut. Bentley in 1795 found only about 100 people on each of the two former islands, while Kadamat was then still uninhabited and unplanted. These three islands were probably occupied by settlers from Ameni. The people of Ameni enjoyed at one time a priority over them, traces of which may be seen in the custom only recently abolished, of deciding cases on the other three islands with the help of Ameni muktessors, and in the authority still possessed by the Ameni Khazi over the Naib Khazis of the other islands.

First settlement.

Robinson II, p. 9.

In 1845 Sir W. Robinson found Kadamat inhabited, but the people were entirely dependent on the people of Ameni. They had not even boats of their own and much of the land had been appropriated by the Ameni islanders who still hold it. There is now a strong movement on Kadamat to repudiate the superiority of Ameni altogether and the Ameni Khazi's authority in particular. It gave rise in 1908 and 1909 to almost the only criminal cases that have ever occurred on the island.

Robinson I, p. 20.

Conversion of Muhammadanism.

Originally Hindus, the islanders, under the influence of Arab traders, were converted to Muhammadanism at some time probably in the fourteenth century, and thus furnish another example of the way in which the Muhammadan religion followed trade and was accepted almost universally by the islands along the Asiatic coasts.

Robinson II, p. 10.

Tradition on the Laccadives ascribes the conversion to an Arab Saint named Ubaid-ulla who is commonly known on all the islands by the title of Munbē Mūliyākā, a Moplah mispronunciation of the words Munbē Mussaliyār Kākā, the first Mussaliyār. It is said that Ubaid-ulla came to Ameni in A.H. 41, but being unable to convert the inhabitants departed to Androth where he was more successful and not only converted the island but established the family which till 1920 held the Khaziship of Androth, an office held in the greatest veneration throughout the islands. The last Khazi in that family professed to be twenty-fourth in direct descent from the Saint.

The Mussaliyār is said next to have converted Kavarathi and Agathi and then to have returned once more to Ameni in A.H. 44. This time he was more successful and converted the whole island. Passing to Kalpeni, he converted that island also. Finally he returned to Androth where he remained until his death. His tomb is in the jamath mosque at Androth and the mosque is in conseqence held in the greatest veneration. It is said that he did not visit Kiltan, Chetlat or Kadamat but that the people of these islands, hearing of the conversion of Ameni, came to that island and were converted by the Saint's agent there. To this circumstance popular tradition ascribes the present subordination of the smaller islands to the Khazi of Ameni in religious affairs. Whatever truth there may be in this account of the saint's life, the dates assigned are obviously impossible: the conversion of the islands can hardly safely be placed earlier than the fourteenth century.

The Portuguese.

The islands appear to have remained independent of the chiefs and rulers on the mainland until after the arrival of the Portuguese on the West Coast. The Portuguese made a settlement upon Ameni and built a fort, the site of which is still pointed out, but their object in doing so is difficult to discern. They seem to have treated the inhabitants with cruelty and harshness. The islanders were driven to seek the assistance of the Raja of Chirakkal. Tradition relates that the Raja sent over Kadantavanjiraka (lit. "Ear-bored") whose identity is lost under his nick name. A plan to poison the Portuguese was formed and the Portuguese were in this way exterminated. This event is still commemorated in the name (Pambupalli) of one of the mosques on Ameni,

Robinson II, p. 67.

where, it is said, the poison was prepared. The Portuguese took a bloody revenge. More than 400 of the islanders, including the Khazi of the day, Abu Bakr, were massacred. The date of this occurrence (A.H. 966. A.D. 1549-50) is fortunately preserved in an old Moplah song in honour of Abu Bakr, who is now regarded as a martyr. Tradition relates two subsequent massacres by the Portuguese of the people of Chetlat.

Chirakkal rule.

In consequence of the Chirakkal Raja's interference in this affair he was eventually enabled to establish his authority over all the islands. He held them for several years and at some unknown date transferred them in jaghir, with the title of Raja, upon the Ali Raja, the head of the Moplah community in Cannanore. The stipulated peshkash was 6,000 fanams a year. This was paid until about the middle of the eighteenth century, when the Cannanore family took advantage of the gradual dismemberment of the Chirakkal territories to assert its own independence. From this time forward the Cannanore and Chirakkal Rajas became inveterate foes and it was on the invitation of the former that Hyder Ali invaded North Malabar in 1765-66 and completed the ruin of the Chirakkal family.

Grant in jaghir to Ali Raja.

Robinson II, p. 11.

Revolt of Amindivi islands, 1784.

The abuses and exactions under Cannanore rule, particularly in connexion with the coir monopoly introduced between 1760-65, drove the northern islands Ameni, Chetlat and Kiltan (Kadamat being uninhabited) to revolt. In 1783 four Ameni boats sailing to Cannanore with island produce found the place blockaded by the English. One boat fell into the hands of the English, another returned to the island, but the remaining two, belonging to the still influential Kulap and Porakat families sailed on to Mangalore, where, under the impression that the Cannanore family was doomed, they disposed of their coir to Tippu, who was himself at the time besieging Mangalore.

Robinson II, p. 68.

On the restoration of peace by the treaty of Mangalore (11th March 1784), the Bibi proceeded to punish with the utmost rigour the offence against her monopoly laws which these two boats had committed. She sent over to Ameni Abdul Khadir Kariyakar with a body of servants. On landing he confiscated and seized the property and persons, and emptied the houses, of the principal inhabitants, a form of punishment known on the islands as Kavarcha. This proved more than the people could stand. The whole population rose, overpowered the guards, released the prisoners and placed Abdul Khadir in chains. The principal inhabitants then sailed to Mangalore taking Abdul Khadir with

A Kavarcha.

them in chains, and offered their allegiance to Tippu. He, however, was by this time once more on friendly terms with the Bibi, and tried to persuade them to return to their allegiance to her. All his endeavours proving unsuccessful, he, at length, in 1787, accepted the offer of the islanders and granted in compensation to the Cannanore family a jaghir from the Chirakkal territories.

Malabar islands ceded to Honourable Company, 1791.

In 1791 the southern islands passed, by the conquest of Cannanore, to the East India Company along with other possessions of the Bibi; and were further ceded, with Tippu's entire possessions in Malabar, by the peace of Seringapatam in 1792. But the northern islands continued in Tippu's possession until the fall of Seringapatam in 1799 when, with Kanara, they passed to the Honourable Company. The accident of the revolt in 1784 thus accounts for the arbitrary division which now places the Amindivis, as they are called, under South Kanara and the southern islands under Malabar for administrative purposes.

Amindivis ceded to Honourable Company, 1799. Robinson II, p. 13.

Upon the fall of Cannanore in 1791, the Chirakkal Raja seized the opportunity to resume the lands granted by Tippu to the Bibi as compensation for the loss of the Amindivis. In 1792 the Bibi, refusing to admit defeat, claimed to be treated like other Rajas of Malabar, but it was pointed out to her that rights of sovereignty had been acquired by the Company over her possessions by conquest, not as in other cases by alliance. It was determined, however, "as a matter of policy and conciliatory of the Mappillas in general" to permit her to retain her possessions, provided she paid a tribute to the Honourable Company. Thereupon commenced a lengthy dispute between the Bibi and the Bombay Government, under which Malabar then was, as to the amount of tribute to be levied. The Bibi asserted that her total income from the southern islands was only Rs. 20,000, while Lieut. Bentley, who was specially deputed in 1795 to visit the islands and report as to their value, estimated the Bibi's probable revenue at Rs. 1,17,699. The question dragged on for years in a lengthy correspondence which is given in full at pages 84-133 of Sir W. Robinson's report of 1848. The Bibi complicated it still further by demanding, in 1793, a remission in lieu of the lands resumed by the Chirakkal Raja. Her own statement of profits had been accepted provisionally in 1793, and she entered into a muchilika to pay the half of it (Rs. 10,000), together with half of such additional profits as might subsequently be discovered, and also to agree to the sequestration of the islands whenever such a course should seem advisable. In 1795, in consequence

Robinson II, pp. 86-100.

Bibi retains possession of Malabar islands.

Dispute as to peshkash.

of a strong report from Lieut. Bentley upon the miserable condition of the islanders under the Bibi's exactions, the Governor-General ordered (27th July 1795) that the coir monopoly must be abolished and some plan for the better management of the islands drawn up, in consultation with the Bibi. The Bibi, however, refused to resign any portion of her sovereignty, or to allow any direct interference with the internal administration of the islands, and on her side raised again the question of her assessment, which had been increased by Rs. 2,000, upon her possessions on the mainland. A compromise was arrived at through the good offices of Mr. Peile, the Principal Collector. An agreement was signed on 30th October 1796, which fixed the assessment at Rs. 10,000 on the Laccadives and also settled some minor matters that had been in dispute. This agreement reiterated the stipulation in the muchilika which reserved to Government the right to sequestrate the islands at any time. No arrangements had been made, however, to give effect to the Governor-General's wishes that the coir monopoly should be abolished. The Governor of Bombay in reviewing the agreement pointed this out and desired that Mr. Peile should be directed to open fresh negotiations for this purpose. Mr. Peile's endeavours were entirely unsuccessful. On 15th September 1797, he was forced to report that not only had every argument proved fruitless but that the Bibi now even repudiated the sequestration clauses in the agreements of 1793 and 1796. She was prepared, however, to allow the Company to appoint some person to administer justice on the islands and she was also prepared to allow some officer to reside on the islands for a year and ascertain their real value. The Bombay Government accepted these two proposals as a temporary measure, as they were averse to taking formal possession of the islands during the war with France, fearing the depredations of French men-of-war. The Commissioners replied (13th February 1798) that they would nominate two persons to proceed to the islands "after the rains," but no further record of the transactions is preserved in the Collector's office.

Bibi claims remission for resumption of land by Chirakkal Raja.

The Bibi's claim to remission on account of the lands recovered by the Chirakkal Raja which had been originally granted to her by Tippu in compensation for the Amindivis, was at first summarily rejected. She continued, however, to revive it at every opportunity. In 1804 she even claimed the restoration of the Amindivis themselves, and although the Bombay Government reported to the Board of Directors that "she had no just claim to be placed in any other situation by

Robinson II, p. 122.

the conquest of Mysore than that in which she would have stood if such an event had not taken place," the Honourable Court of Directors (6th December 1805) took a different view, and held that "although from the aversion of the inhabitants to the Government of the Bibi it may not be advisable to restore those islands to her, some consideration in money should be allowed her on account of them as it was no doubt the protection of the British which enabled the Raja of Chirakkal to resume or keep without a struggle the grants made to the Bibi by Tippu in compensation for the loss of the Amindivis." The amount of compensation, reckoned at half the net revenue from the islands was finally (6th April 1807) fixed by the Principal Collector at 1,500 Star Pagodas (Rs. 5,250). The Bibi appears to have rejected this as inadequate. Intermediate correspondence on the matter is missing. The next record extant is the final report from the Board of Revenue to the Chief Secretary, dated 3rd October 1822, upon which the Government ordered an annual abatement of Rs. 5,250 from the assessment due by the Cannanore family. This sum continued to be deducted until 1908 when it merged in the malikhana granted under the agreement then made with the Cannanore Raja.

Government waives its claim to the sovereignty. Robinson II, p. 180.

The attitude taken up by the Bibi in 1795 upon the question of sovereignty was strongly maintained ever afterwards. The sequestration clause in the muchilika of 1793 and in the agreement of 1796 was never enforced, and when the question was raised once again in 1847, Government decided "not to take advantage of it to put an end to a possession for so many years tacitly acquiesced in." The policy of Government with reference to the islands in subsequent years was seriously restricted by this magnanimous decision. It was at once found impossible to obtain the introduction of the much needed reforms, suggested by Sir W. Robinson as a result of his visit to the islands in 1847, and, although the islands were attached for ten years (1854—1864) for arrears of peshkash, the only reform effected was the abolition of some of the minor monopolies. Sultan Ali Raja, the head of the Cannanore family when the islands were next visited by a British officer (Mr. Logan) in 1869, had lost all control over the islands of Agathi, Androth and Kavarathi and his authority was recognised in Kalpeni only to a very limited extent. The object of Mr. Logan's visit was to ascertain how the Raja's authority could be strengthened and his administration improved, yet so jealous was the Raja of all interference, that he put every possible obstruction in Mr. Logan's way to prevent his obtaining information. Mr. Logan traced the trouble to the monopoly system and the abuses it gave rise

Consequent difficulties.

Logans' report, 1869.

to, and suggested the abolition of all monopolies. Government approved, but the Raja refused to accept the proposal and instead claimed a salute of guns and an hereditary title. G.O. 405, Pol., 20th Dec. 1871.

Anarchy on Malabar islands.

While the matter was still being discussed, the state of anarchy on the islands continued to increase. No monopoly articles were shipped to Cannanore ; Government refused the Raja's request that they would assist him to enforce the monopoly by arms ; the Raja derived practically no income from the islands ; and on 3rd April 1875 it became necessary to attach them again for arrears. This attachment remained in force until 1908 when the Bibi surrendered her phantom sovereignty. Its object was not merely to clear off the arrears of peshkash, but also, and mainly, to afford an opportunity for introducing the much needed reforms in the administrative and fiscal systems. The Raja was plainly told that the islands would not be handed back to him until their administration had been placed upon a sound basis, and, more particularly, until some other system had been substituted for that of the monopolies.

Attachment, 1875—1908. G.O. 416, Pol., 2nd July 1877.

Difficulty of administration.

The position was not without difficulty. The introduction of reforms was hindered by the fact that Government was only administering the islands in trust for the Raja. Successive Collectors, impressed with the difficulties that thus arose, recommended the absolute confiscation of the islands, pointing out that the people had been from the first entirely opposed to any rendition to the Raja and were prepared to resist to the utmost any attempt on his part to re-establish his authority. It was shown that there was little hope that the arrears of peshkash would ever be cleared and still less that the Raja would be able to carry on any system of administration that might be introduced ; while a recurrence of the previous abuses would only mean another attachment of the islands in the not distant future. This view was accepted, and in 1889 the Government of Madras recommended the assumption of the sovereignty over the islands under the treaties of 1793 and 1796. The Government of India, however, maintained their previous attitude and found it impossible to accept the Madras Government's proposal. In 1895 the question attracted the attention of the Government at Home and Sir H. Fowler, the then Secretary of State for India, ordered the immediate rendition of the sovereignty to the Raja if he cleared the arrears.

G.O. 544, Pol., 12th Sep. 1892.

This—one may venture to think fortunately—was found to be beyond the Raja's powers and became with every year more and more impossible, for the arrears were gradually accumulating, and by 1908, with interest, had reached the sum of Rs. 2,17,162.

Negotiations for surrender of sovereignty.

In 1900 negotiations were opened with the Raja to induce him to surrender the claim to a sovereignty, which, it was pointed out, he could now never hope to exercise, but he absolutely refused the terms offered. The same terms, modified, so far as possible, to meet his wishes, were offered to him again in 1905 with the intimation that if he did not choose to accept them, Government would assume the sovereignty upon their own terms, which indeed were sufficiently liberal, for they guaranteed that although, while continuing to administer the islands, Government would cease to credit the profits to the Raja and to grant him the Amindivi compensation, they would remit all arrears of peshkash, he on his part paying a peshkash of Rs. 3,617 on his Karar lands on the mainland, about which, on the introduction of the Malabar Settlement, there had also been disputes.

The Raja, Muhammad Ali, preferred to accept the terms proposed by Government, which were: that all arrears of peshkash should be remitted; that the payment of the Amindivi compensation should cease; that he should receive a malikhana of Rs. 23,000 to be paid to the Raja and his successors, one-half as a personal grant to the head of the family, and the other half for the use and benefit of the family; that he should hold free of all peshkash or assessment the disputed Karar lands on the mainland; and that he should receive the hereditary title of Sultan.

Sovereignty relinquished.

Unfortunately before a formal agreement could be drawn up Muhammad Ali died in 1907 and the whole question had to be reopened in 1908 with his successor, Impichi Bibi, who was at first inclined to repudiate Muhammad Ali's virtual acceptance, but finally agreed to the terms offered by Government. The agreement was signed on the 15th November 1908 at Cannanore by the Bibi and by Mr. Francis, Collector of Malabar, on behalf of the Governor-General. It was ratified by the Governor-General on 5th February 1909 and the necessary proclamations were published in the *Gazette of India* of 6th February 1909. It should be noted that under this agreement the islands form part of His Majesty's Indian dominions as from 1st July 1905.

Ends a curious situation.

This liberal agreement, the result of a desire on the part of Government to put once more "upon its feet" the old Mappilla House of Cannanore, put an end to a curious anomaly arising out of a decision of the High Court (I.L.R., Madras XIII, 353). In 1889, in consequence of friction at Androth between the Kunnangalath family represented by K. Cheriya Koya, subsequently Amin of Androth, and the Chamayath family, one of whose members Saiyid Ahamed Koya was then Amin, serious breaches of the peace occurred upon the island.

In December 1889, Mr. Twigg, then Sub-Collector of Malabar, was sent with a body of Police in H.M.S. *Criffon* to hold an inquiry. As a result, he convicted Cheriya Koya and others of the Kunnangalath faction of the offences of rioting, causing hurt and committing affray, and also bound them over to keep the peace. Mr. Twigg had acted in his executive capacity as Sub-Collector but had followed the provisions of the Penal and Criminal Procedure Codes. His decisions were appealed against to the High Court. It does not seem to have been brought to the notice of the High Court that the sovereignty of the islands had never been assumed by the British Government and the learned judges merely stated, in a short preliminary sketch of the way in which the Honourable Company obtained possession, that by the peace of Seringapatam in 1792 the islands, "became an integral portion of the territories which vested in Her Majesty by the Statute 21 and 22 Vic., Cap. 106" although they noticed that "a large share of administrative independence in their internal affairs was, till the year 1875, left in the hands of the Bibi." The entry "Laccadive islands, including Minicoy" in the first schedule to the Scheduled Districts Act seemed to confirm their view and they held that as the islands had not been exempted under that Act from the operations of the Indian Penal Code and Criminal Procedure Code, those Codes must be in force. It was held, therefore, that Mr. Twigg had acted without authority and that his proceedings were void *ab initio*.

The difference in status between the Malabar Laccadives and the Amindivis seems to have escaped the notice even of Government at the time when the Scheduled Districts Act was drawn up, for the entry in the first schedule of that Act should, of course, have referred only to the South Kanara islands. The position legally, however, on the islands became in consequence of this decision of the High Court somewhat curious. In the eye of the law the Malabar islands formed a part of British India, while actually they did not, and although every judicial proceeding held on the islands was in danger of being quashed by the High Court, there was no course open to Government but to issue confidential orders to ignore the High Court ruling and to administer justice as before. The islands by Notification No. 227 of the Home Department, Government of India, dated 1st February 1912, were formally incorporated in the Madras Presidency, while by Notification No. 228 of the same date they were placed under the jurisdiction of the Madras High Court.

The first authentic information about the Laccadives was gathered by Lieut. Bentley, who visited the Malabar group in 1795 under circumstances already detailed. His short and rather summary report, which is still extant, is mainly statistical and is consequently of but little interest. The islands were not again visited until Mr. (afterwards Sir) W. Robinson visited the Amindivis in 1845 and the Malabar islands two years later. His two very full reports give a most interesting account of the islands at that time and bring out very clearly the difference between the condition of the Amindivi islanders under British rule and that of the other islanders under Cannanore mismanagement.

Condition of Malabar islands, 1847. Robinson II, pp. 32–36.

Robinson II, p. 38.

Monopoly of exports. Robinson II, p. 40.

The condition of the Malabar islanders had indeed become wretched. A sharp fall in the price of coir in 1826, from Rs. 60 to Rs. 20 per candy, had forced the Cannanore Rajas to reduce the price paid for the article, which was their monopoly, and other changes had also been introduced, with the consequence that the people were being paid at the rate of Rs. 6-6-0 per candy for their staple product, while the people on the Government islands were receiving Rs. 18-8-0 per candy. In many years, indeed, the people were not paid at all for much of the coir or were paid by credit orders at the rate of 7 fanams (Rs. 1-6-0) per muda of rice, the average price of rice being then Rs. 1-8-0 per muda. Again, in enforcing the monopoly on coconuts, which did not exist on the Amindivis, the Raja paid Rs. 5 per 1,000 (the average value on the coast being Rs. 7-9-0 per 1,000) and also deducted an import duty of 10 per cent and made large allowances for small or bad nuts. So oppressive was this monopoly felt to be that smuggling had become rife. Except jaggery, all the minor products of the islands, cowries, tortoise-shell, trepang, etc., were also monopolised, and the terms granted to the islanders were as unfair and vexatious as in the case of the larger monopolies. The profits on the cowry monopoly amounted to 400 per cent. Even the manufacture of jaggery did not wholly escape, for the toddy drawers had to pay heavy presents to the officials on the islands. All breaches of monopoly were most severely punished.

And of imports.

Robinson II, p. 46.

Forced by this monopoly system to sell all their exports to the Raja, at the arbitrary prices he chose to fix, the people's condition would have been miserable enough. But not content with the considerable profits thus accruing to him, the Raja maintained a strict monopoly of all the import trade as well. He forced the islanders to purchase commodities at his own price and to pay him in coir, supplying them with inferior rice and inferior tobacco, and using, it is almost superfluous to add, weights that favoured him by 2 or 3 lb. in every maund of 32 lb. The tobacco trade was particulary scandalous,

The price of a bundle of 3 maunds at Mahē was Rs. 12, but the islanders were forced to give in exchange 40 maunds of coir per bundle at Rs. 65 per candy in the earlier years and 75 maunds at Rs. 20 per candy at the time of Sir W. Robinson's visit. The profits thus secured varied from 500 to 1,000 per cent. But the great hardship in the whole proceeding was that the people had no option whether to buy or not. It was found impossible to check smuggling except by importing a large quantity of tobacco and then compelling every one to receive a share. When the tobacco arrived, the chief men of each division were given the share to be distributed in their respective divisions, and they in their turn had to distribute this share among the rest of the people. The requirements of the people were not considered at all, care only being taken to see that they were supplied with more than they actually needed, so that there might be no temptation to smuggle. Again, monopolising as he did the whole of the produce of the islands, the Raja was necessarily the only person from whom the islanders could obtain loans or advances, and he took every advantage of the situation. Advances of rice or other articles were made for coir at retail monopoly prices on the islands. Accounts were kept in terms of bundles of coir and then converted into money at the market value of the coir. Two sets of accounts were kept, one on the islands for recent transactions, and the other at Cannanore for old outstanding balances. Judicial fines and penalties for breaches of monopoly, arrears of rent, fees for the grant of titles and upon accession to the Khaziship, in fact arrears of almost any kind, seem to have been carried to account against the various families. Nothing was ever written off as irrecoverable, and this balance of debt went on accumulating from year to year, until, at the time of Sir W. Robinson's visit, the indebtedness was so universal that 10 per cent of all coir imported to Cannanore was compulsorily deducted by the Raja as a set off.

Compulsory imports of tobacco.

Universal indebtedness to the Raja.

Robinson II, p. 47.

The discontent of the Cannanore islanders was naturally increased by contrast of their condition with that of the Amindivi islanders under British rule. The administration of the northern islands was conducted on much the same lines then as now, and the people enjoyed, except in famine years, a fair measure of prosperity. The coir monopoly was worked fairly and gave a sufficient return for their labour, although, owing to the low price of coir and the cheapness of rice, the system did not then yield the profits that were subsequently derived from it. There was no monopoly upon coconuts. Tortoise shell, ambergris and cowries were monopolised

Contrasted condition of Amindivi islanders.

Robinson II, p. 134.

as on the Malabar islands but, except a tax on salt, there was no restriction upon other trade. The Malabar islanders naturally clamoured also to be taken under British rule, and feeling against the Raja grew more and more intense on the islands. Government could do but little without a departure from their policy of recognising the Raja's independence. In 1859, however, while the islands were under Government management, the coconut, morinda citron, lime, tobacco, and salt monopolies, and the fees paid by pilots, were abolished upon the representations made by the Board of Revenue on Sir W. Robinson's reports.

Since the final attachment in 1875 little history has been made upon the islands. The people are wonderfully quiet and law-abiding and the only disturbances of the public peace which have to be recorded since the islands came under British management have been those at Androth in 1889 already referred to, and riots on Minicoy in 1887 and 1912 which might have had serious consequences.

Disturbances on Minicoy in 1887.

The causes of the trouble at Minicoy in 1887 are obscure. Mr. Dance had visited the island in December 1884 to appoint a successor as Amin to the famous Dom Ali Malikhan, the richest man in Minicoy, who with his little fleet monopolised Minicoy trade, and who is still remembered throughout the Laccadives as the "Capithan." The people's choice rested upon Bodugothi Ali Malikhan in preference to Dom Malikhan's brother. Mr. Dance returned to Minicoy in the "May Frere" in January 1885 and attempted to issue cowles for the Pandaram lands, in accordance with the system already successfully introduced by Mr. Logan upon the other islands. Only 3 men, however, agreed to take cowles. The rest of the islanders stubbornly refused to have anything to do with the innovation. In January 1887, Mr. Logan himself accompanied Mr. Dance to Minicoy, expecting to be able to reason the islanders into accepting his scheme. Mr. Logan, however, at once found that any attempt to parcel out the Big South Pandaram on cowle must be abandoned. Mr. Logan returned to Calicut after explaining to the people that cowles would not be introduced, leaving Mr. Dance with orders to clear the screw-pine jungle in the Big South Pandaram, as a first step in the extermination of the rats which, then as now, caused incalculable damage to the coconuts. The people, however, proved as determined in their opposition to the clearing of the jungle as they had been to the introduction of the cowles. Mr. Dance attempted to reason with them, but they always fell back upon the answer that it was contrary to custom, and that it would be necessary to kill or transport them before the jungle could be cleared.

Next day (February 10th) Mr. Dance could get no coolies to help with the survey. He went with the Amin into the village and found the islanders assembled at their different meeting places. He went to where the Takrus were assembled, having heard that they were the most troublesome, and asked for 20 coolies, informing the headman that if the coolies were not sent, the headman would be imprisoned for obstructing the officers of Government. He then left, but had hardly gone 20 yards when the whole assembly rushed upon his little party, shouting that they would kill the Amin. Mr. Dance placed himself in front of the Amin, and, with the assistance of his two peons who pluckily stood their ground, held the crowd back. No attempt appears to have been made to strike Mr. Dance but the crowd kept trying to hit at the Amin behind him. After some minutes Mr. Dance succeeded in pacifying the islanders and told them, if they had any grievance, to come to the cutcherry and represent it quietly, but that for the present he must have the coolies. Coolies were given him and he was allowed to go.

In the evening, a large noisy crowd came to the cutcherry with a petition, demanding the dismissal of the Amin. Mr. Dance insisted that he would only discuss the matter with the headmen, and after considerable difficulty succeeded in getting the crowd to withdraw a short distance from the cutcherry. Mr. Dance told the headmen he required time until next day to consider their request. With very great difficulty he extracted a promise from them that they would prevent any disturbance until then, but they gave him clearly to understand that, if he did not eventually accede to their request, there would certainly be a riot. Indeed when the headmen returned to the crowd and reported the result of their interview with Mr. Dance, the attitude of the islanders became so threatening that Mr. Dance and Capt. Mitchell, R.I.M., decided to disperse them at once, and pluckily went among them, and, with the greatest difficulty, succeeded in getting them to go away.

Later in the evening Mr. Dance received information that the islanders proposed to detain him on the island until he dismissed the Amin. As he had not a sufficient force with him to repel them in the event of an attack or to enforce his authority, he withdrew to the steamer under cover of night, taking with him only the Government records and maps, and of necessity leaving behind his own personal property and the Government treasure box, which was in the Amin's house in the village and could not be secured in time.

Next morning (February 11th) he sailed to Calicut for assistance. Government, by wire, ordered Mr. Logan to return to the island with Mr. Dance, the Assistant Superintendent of Police, Malappuram, Mr. Baudry, and 100 men of the Special Force, to restore order. The order was received by wire at Malappuram at 8 p.m. on the 15th, yet Mr. Baudry had his men all in Calicut by 9-30 next morning with their baggage and equipment, a most creditable performance. Mr. Dance, who had been sent to Madras to explain matters personally to Government, returned on the 16th evening, and the Collector sailed for Minicoy on the 17th. The Government treasure and Mr. Dance's things were found untouched, and no further disturbance of any kind was attempted.

Their causes. At the enquiry which Mr. Logan at once proceeded to hold, no cause for the people's conduct was at all clearly established. Mr. Logan seems to have thought that the outcry against the clearance of the jungle was a mere pretence, and that the whole affair was organized by Dom Malikhan, the late Amin's brother, in order to secure the dismissal of the newly appointed Amin, who had undoubtedly done his best to undermine Dom Malikhan's monopoly of the island trade, by arranging with a wealthy Cutch firm to establish an agency on Minicoy. The Amin had even gone so far as to repair the old Pandaram ship, Hydrose, and send her to the Maldives with a cargo belonging to the Cutch merchant, crediting to Government a freightage of about a fourth of the amount which he debited for repairs. The opposition to the clearance of the jungle collapsed dramatically as soon as Dom Malikhan admitted that he was not opposed to it, and it is remarkable that the Takrus, the class most dependent upon Dom Malikhan, were almost the only section of the people who had opposed Mr. Dance's orders in the matter. Government commended Mr. Dance for his courage and prudence, but considered that he should not have left the island before passing orders, as he had promised to do. So ended the affair, but the question of introducing the cowle system, or of substituting a tree tax for the poll tax and tax on fishing boats, was indefinitely postponed.

In 1912. The next trouble on Minicoy arose in 1912 when Mr. Doig, the Inspecting Officer that year, was faced with a very similar situation. He found the whole island clamouring for the removal of an unpopular Amin. He was even threatened with detention on the island until he should dismiss the Amin, and thought it wisest to get away from the island as quietly as possible and secure police assistance from Calicut. Mr. C. A. Innes, the Collector, with a force of Reserve police, returned with him to the island and held an enquiry. The real grounds for the strong feeling against the Amin were never fully discovered, but it seems highly probable that, as in 1887, the question of the Great South Pandaram led to the revolt of the people against authority. Although the South Pandaram was Government property and Government through the Amin was taking the coconut crop produced from it, the people possessed certain very valuable communal rights in it, as regards the cutting of timber and the taking of cadjans for thatching, and also received very large remuneration in the shape of mamuls for their help in plucking the nuts. There can be little doubt that successive Amins had been forced to allow a distribution of nuts considerably in excess of the mamuls, or that they themselves took a good share of the total produce. It is impossible otherwise to account for the steady decline in the total of nuts plucked each year, and, when it is remembered that the people have almost no land of their own and that the Pandaram includes nearly all the planted area of the island, the temptations will be obvious. Attempts had been made by the Inspecting Officers in 1908 and 1909 to impress upon the Amin the necessity for a strict adherence to the mamuls, and threats were held out that if an improvement was not shown some other arrangement would have to be made. Some effect was produced by these means. The number of nuts plucked increased considerably in the next two years. But the people were determined, apparently, to break an Amin who should attempt to be honest and deprive them of their unauthorised mamuls. The result was a conspiracy against the Amin which broke out upon Mr. Doig's arrival.

Mr. Innes' first care, upon reaching the islands, was to re-establish authority, which he succeeded in doing without difficulty. He then set about enquiring into the grievances against the Amin. Having satisfied himself that they originated almost entirely out of the management of the South Pandaram, he began to consider the possibility of establishing some other system. He was much impressed with the injustice of the old system, received from the Bibi's time, by which nearly the whole planted area of the island was the monopoly of Government, and the people's legitimate share in the produce only some exiguous mamuls. It was obvious too that there could be no check upon the honesty of the Amin and the people, and that, when they chose to combine, Government was at their mercy, while when the Amin tried to be honest he had to face the united opposition of the whole island. The people had always refused to allow individuals to accept cowles in the Pandaram, and Mr. Innes found them still equally opposed to that course. He decided that the only alternative was to hand over the whole Pandaram to them in common, on a rental of Rs. 1,552 to be revised after 30 years. The people willingly accepted this decision. It constituted an extremely liberal settlement which proved beneficial in every way. A perpetual cause of unrest was removed and peace and tranquillity have reigned on the island since. The people secured a very valuable property which they at once set about managing and improving. They are no strangers to co-operative principles and thus were peculiarly fitted to manage their new property successfully. In imitation of the old Sirkar administration a special Pandaram Amin and peons were appointed. The Amin holds office for one year and with the Attiri Muppans administers the Pandaram. Under his control each Attiri has its own section of the Pandaram to attend to. Immediately the condition of the Pandaram altered strikingly. Under the old regime the ground beneath the trees was covered with a mass of screw-pine jungle, there were only a few main paths, and planting took place spasmodically for a year or two at long intervals and then only in the portion nearest the village. Now the jungle is being cleared, good paths cut, and planting is being regularly attended to by each Attiri in its own section. After division of a portion of the proceeds, a communal fund has been formed with the balance, and already, out of this fund, one of the old Minicoy brigs, which used to belong to the famous Dom Malikhan, has been purchased from his successors, repaired, and sailed to Madras and Calcutta on a co-operative trading enterprise. There can be little doubt that with their industry and capacity the islanders will eventually make the Pandaram a very valuable property indeed. The Pandaram Amin is already for his term of office the most influential man on the island. The rise of this new official of the people, combined with the already powerful organisation of the Attiris, has resulted in the reduction of the Sirkar Amin to an unfortunately subordinate position, while it has become impossible to secure the attendance at Court of the Cutcherry Muppans or any candidates for vacancies among them.

The great war. The German Cruiser *Emden* operated off the Laccadives for a short time in September and October 1914 and sank several vessels on the trade routes which run north and south of Minicoy. Several life boats and some wreckage belonging to the vessels sunk were washed up on Kalpeni.

Inspections. After Sir W. Robinson's visit in 1847, more than 20 years elapsed before the Malabar Laccadives were again visited by a British officer (Mr. Logan in 1869). The Amindivis had been visited by Mr. Sewell three years previously. Government repeatedly resolved that the island should be visited at least biennially, but the greatest difficulty was found in obtaining a ship to take the Inspecting Officer out, and it was only for a few years subsequent to 1902 that visits were made with any regularity. A list of Inspecting Officers is given in Appendix IV.

The earlier visits were made under not the most comfortable conditions. Mr. Sewell in 1866 had to charter and provision a pattamar for his visit. The little *Margaret Northcote* made many of the earlier voyages. One advantage of her small size was that she could enter the lagoons and anchor close inshore, but she carried no reserve of coal. Coal recovered from wrecks at Kalpeni was very largely used in some years. Trips made in her possessed an unpleasant element of uncertainty. On one occasion her engines broke down and she was only just worked back to Calicut. On another, in November 1881, she altogether failed to make Minicoy. The ship was sent out with a faulty chronometer and after failing to make the island was forced to return for want of water. Her captain indeed seems to have been fortunate in making the mainland again at all, for Mr. Underwood writes "when the chronometer was taken on board H.M.S. *Ready* to be rated, the Captain and Navigating Lieutenant were pleased to be facetious over it and presumed it was only because the continent was in the way that we had not gone to Rangoon." Eventually she reached Minicoy.

Incidents of earlier inspections.

Failure to find Minicoy.

Similar difficulties were experienced on the trips made in later years by the *Marguerita*, subsequently employed on the Tuticorin Pearl Fisheries. She too once failed to find Minicoy, although by that time (1895) a light house had been erected on the island; and, after steaming in all directions for 24 hours without sighting the island, was forced to return. The printed reports record no reason for this misadventure.

Purchase of a steam yacht proposed.

In 1891, the B.I.S.N. *Kistna* was chartered to take Mr. Hewetson, the Collector, who himself inspected the islands that year. In view of the expense entailed, Mr. Hewetson recommended the purchase of a suitable steam yacht for the use of the Collector, and his proposal was supported by the Board and repeated again by the Board in 1893, but action was deferred by Government as the question of the future administration of the islands was then under discussion with the Secretary of State. In 1892 the Indian Marine S.S. *Outram* was placed at the disposal of Government for the inspection, but in 1893 and again in 1895 no Indian Marine vessel was available and recourse was had once more to the *Marguerita*. In 1898 it was found impossible to obtain any vessel except at prohibitive cost, and the visit arranged for that year had to be given up. In 1900 the R.I.M.S. *Elphinstone* was placed at the disposal of Government. Finally in 1901 it was ordered by the Government of India (vide G.O. No. 547, Revenue, dated 27th June 1901) that in future an R.I.M. ship would be placed annually at the disposal of the Madras Government for the inspection trip. From that date until the Great War broke out, annual inspections were made except in the years 1903, 1910 and 1911, when again no R.I.M. steamers were available. The outbreak of war and the consequent impossibility of securing a ship prevented further inspection till 1920, with the exception of a short visit by Mr. Evans in 1916 to Minicoy and Androth, which was made from Colombo in the Board of Trade Lights steamer.

The R.I.M. to furnish a steamer annually.

The great importance of an annual inspection of the islands has long been recognised but the impossibility of obtaining a ship in each year has so far prevented this from being done. The result of the war was to make it impossible for the R.I.M. to carry out the orders of 1901. It has been promised that in future, provided the Madras Government gives sufficient notice an R.I.M. ship will be placed at its disposal for the inspection, but the difficulties and failures of past years leave little hope that it will always be possible to fulfil the promise. Other alternatives have been proposed from time to time. In 1918-19 the proposal to build a joint inspection steamer and trawler for the Fisheries Department was very thoroughly examined by a Committee, and sanctioned plans for the proposed steamer were sent to England for execution, but the proposal had to be dropped owing to the prohibitive cost of construction at post-war rates. In connexion with the inspection of 1920 enquiries were made in Colombo as to the possibility of chartering a steamer there for the trip. It was found that steamers belonging to Messrs. Walker & Co., Colombo, and also the Ceylon Government trawlers, could be made available by arrangement but the necessity to proceed further in the matter was obviated by the R.I.M. being able to place the *Minto* on duty for the inspection. In 1922, the inspection was made in the *Lady Nicholson*, belonging to the Fisheries Department. She performed the service quite satisfactorily and if she can be made available for the inspection in future years, the difficult problem of finding a suitable ship would appear to have been solved.

Wrecks.

Situated as they are in the line of navigation from the Cape to Bombay or Colombo to Aden or Bombay, shipwrecks have been frequent upon these low-lying islands. The following is a list:—

1828. The *Byramgore* bound from China to Bombay laden with silver, silks, etc., was lost on the reef to which she has given her name.

1844. The *Ceylon*, England to Bombay, was wrecked on Cheriyapani reef. All the crew were lost. Sir W. Robinson, then Head Assistant, was sent to recover the cargo and succeeded in salving a very large part of it. He very generously invested Rs. 4,000, presented to him as salvage fees, in Government paper and set it apart as an island Charity Fund for the support of destitute islanders. The fund now amounts to Rs. 9,000 and supports from 10 to 12 islanders.

1853. The *Vizier* bound from England to Bombay was wrecked on Cheriyapani. Her cargo, piece-goods, cotton stuffs, cutlery, etc., was lost but the crew succeeded in reaching Chetlat where they lived for some months before being taken off. On Chetlat Carpenter Primrose died and a tombstone was subsequently erected over his grave by the crew of the *General Simpson* in 1863. It has recently been repaired by the Monegar.

1854. The *Homidy*, an Arab ship bound from Bombay to Mauritius, was lost on Byramgore, but the crew and part of the cargo were saved.

The *Mohomed*, a pilgrim ship from the Malabar Coast, went ashore at Ameni, through carelessness while shifting her anchorage, and was lost, but fortunately the crew and pilgrims were all saved. It is believed that the two old guns which ornament the platform in front of the cutcherry at Ameni belonged to this ship.

1858. The *Alchemist* from England to Bombay and the *Sultan*, Mauritius to Bombay were both lost on Byramgore.

1863. The *General Simpson*, bound from Bombay to England with cotton, was lost on Chetlat.

1864. The *Tutch Rusack* sent to salve the *General Simpson*, approaching Chetlat at night, ran on the reef and was lost.

1865. The *Lord Brougham* was lost on Cheriyapani and the *Abel Tasman*, a Dutch ship bound from Bombay to London, was wrecked on Byramgore, set on fire and abandoned.

1880. The *Amelia* was lost on Kalpeni. Coal recovered from her was long used by the small inspection steamers. Her boilers were washed up on to the reef by the Cyclone of 1922.

1881. The *Mahableshwar* was lost off the Bangaram reef during the monsoon. The crew succeeded in escaping to Bangaram where they lived for about three months until discovered by the Agathi Islanders on visiting Bangaram after the close of the monsoon. Rough calendars cut Crusoe fashion on some trees on Bangaram can still be seen and the wreck itself is still visible in calm weather.

1899. The *Thrunscoe* was lost off the north-east end of the Minicoy reef.

1909. The *Duffryn Manor* bound from Colombo to London was lost in almost the same position. She was a new ship returning home on her first voyage, laden with rice which was freely presented to the islanders and jettisoned, in the hope of lightening the ship sufficiently to get her off. The islanders received almost a five years' supply of rice and actually commenced to export it. The ship's accommodation ladder for some years adorned the Minicoy jetty, while a big cast iron bath was installed in the cutcherry for the use of the Inspecting Officer.

1910. The *Delagoa*, a Swedish steamer bound from Colombo to Europe, stranded on the north, east end of the island, and became a total wreck.

1911. The *Beachy* chartered by the P. & O. Company to carry a cargo of goods for the Delhi Darbar went ashore in December at almost the same spot as the two preceding ships. Among her cargo was some of the King's State harness and about 40 tons of fireworks for the Darbar celebrations. The ship was lightened by salvage parties from Colombo and was eventually got off but the cargo arrived too late for the Darbar.

It is interesting to note that all the wrecks before 1865 occurred on the northern islands and reefs, and that, synchronising with the change in the trade route to India which followed upon the opening of the Suez Canal and with the wider application of steam to shipping, wrecks on those islands ceased entirely from that year, while the few wrecks subsequently have occurred on the southern islands, no less than three of them being on Minicoy alone, which lies directly in the present trade routes from Colombo to Aden or Bombay.

Minicoy Lighthouse. The location of a lighthouse on Minicoy was decided upon in 1882. The building was actually commenced in 1883 and finished in 1885. The lighthouse is 160 feet high and the light is visible for 19 miles. Along with the Basses lighthouse off the Ceylon coast, it is under the direct control of the Board of Trade, London, and is in charge of the Superintendent, Imperial Light Service, Colombo, who visits Minicoy every six months in the Board of Trade tender *Ceylon* to relieve the light-keepers and to replenish their oil and stores. Minicoy islanders are granted free passages in the *Ceylon* to and from the island under certain restrictions. The transfer of the lighthouse to the Government of India is under consideration.

CHAPTER III.

ADMINISTRATION AND REVENUE.

The form of Government which prevailed on the islands in early times appears to have been patriarchal. Authority seems to have vested on each island in a Muthalal who was assisted by the heads of the principal families (Mookyasthans) as a kind of panchayat. In Ameni there existed a council of the four principal families, which had some authority over Chetlat, Kiltan and Kadamat but otherwise each island was independent. This system seems to have continued until some time after the islands came under the power of the Cannanore Rajas. The Rajas at first managed the islands through the Muthalals but subsequently appointed their own agents, known as Kariyakars, upon each island. These men were supposed to act in conjunction with the Mookyasthans or Karanavars as they are now called. Each Kariyakar was assisted by an accountant and 3 or 4 nadpals or peons. As no Raja ever visited the islands, there could be no control whatever over the Kariyakars and it can easily be imagined how greatly they abused their power. Their salary was small, 24 mudas of rice (Rs. 36) per annum, but they were allowed to levy a cess upon the islanders. The Kariyakar himself had to pay the Raja a nazeranah of Rs. 30 upon appointment, and a similar fine for the renewal of his purwana every time he quitted the island. With other fines and fees to the palace officials, the expenses attending the appointment were well known to exceed the salary attached to it. The Kariyakar necessarily depended upon what he could exact from the people, so much of the fish caught, a quarter of every bullock killed, fees on imprisonments and releases, on pilots, on the launch of a new boat. These exactions eventually came to be levied at a fixed rate and the accountant and nadpals claimed their share in strict proportion. When the Kariyakars happened to be islanders their official remuneration was reduced by half, but they seem to have had no compunction in levying the difference off their fellow-islanders and the islanders fared as badly under one of themselves as under a mainlander.

Early form of Government.

Robinson II, p. 11.

Robinson I, p. 16.

Under the Cannanore Rajas.

Robinso II, p. 50.

Exaction by the Kariyakars.

On the South Kanara Islands, the single Kariyakar who had administered the group from Ameni was replaced, when the islands came under British administration by a Monegar resident on Ameni, assisted by a karani or clerk, with

Present administration on South Kanara Islands.

Robinson I, p. 39. peons, permanently stationed on each of the smaller islands. The system has continued to the present time but, with improvement in the class of men holding the office, the powers of the monegar have been increased. In 1845 he had the powers of an Amin, of Police, while disputes of a civil nature were decided by the Karanavars or the Khazi. In 1863 a sub-monegar was appointed for Chetlat, but as he abused his powers and allowed his authority to clash with that of the monegar, the post was abolished in 1867 and the monegar was invested with the powers of a village magistrate and village munsif as defined in Regulations XI of 1816, IV of 1821, and IV and V of 1816. He also had power to inflict fines under the Cattle Trespass Act. In 1871 the pay of the post was raised to Rs. 70 and in 1872 the monegar was invested with the powers of a Third-class Magistrate "provided that in cases beyond his jurisdiction under Regulation XI of 1816 and within his summary jurisdiction as Third-class Magistrate he shall associate with himself as assessors not less than three of the Karanavars of the island in which the trial is held, who shall record their view of the evidence, etc., apart from the monegar's finding." It was pointed out, however, by Mr. Hall in his report for 1874 that the monegar's duties were so multifarious and he was required by custom to exercise authority in so many ways outside the scope of the Civil Procedure Code and the Regulations, that the result of binding him down to laws would be to curtail his power to the verge of uselessness and upset a form of Government which the people were accustomed to and found sufficient. The Scheduled Districts Act (XIV of 1874) was extended to "the Laccadives" by Notification No. 83, Judicial, dated 19th February 1889. This notification, of course, could only apply to the Amindivis, the Malabar Islands not then forming a part of British India. But no notifications under section 3 of the Act were made. In consequence, the High Court held (I.L.R. 13 Mad., p. 353) that both the Indian Penal Code and the Criminal Procedure Code are in force on the Amindivis. The monegar is therefore now appointed a Deputy Tahsildar and in virtue of his office exercises Third-class powers under the Criminal Procedure Code, and appeals and revision petitions lie as laid down in the Code. He also tries a number of more serious offences such as defamation and adultery, under the customary laws, and exercises Civil powers under Madras Regulation, IV of 1816. The present monegar is assisted by a gumastah on Ameni with a resident peon or karani on each of the other islands. The monegar is required to visit the other islands at least three times a year. The karanies have no powers

G.O. No. 2045. 2nd Sep. 1867

G.O. No. 186, 30th Jan. 1872.

G.O. No. 186, 30th January 1872.

and act simply as channels of communication between the monegar and the other islands while he is absent at Ameni. They report to him for orders and carry out the orders when received.

Laws in force on the Amindivis.

By Notification No. 268, dated 9th July 1889, the State Prisoners' Act (XXXIV of 1850 and III of 1858) by Notification, No. 285, dated 4th July 1898, the Lunacy Act, XXXV of 1858) and by Notification No. 197, Judicial, dated 11th February 1909, sections 36 to 43 of the Civil Procedure Code were made applicable to the South Kanara Islands. But the State Prisoners' Regulation (II of 1819) is not in force (G.O. No. 2662, dated 13th August 1910).

On the Malabar islands.

On the Malabar islands the system of administration by Kariyakars nominally prevailed until 1875. After the islands were released in 1864 from the first attachment, the Raja continued to be represented by an agent on each island but his authority was not recognised by the islanders who were by that time in more or less open revolt. Upon the last attachment in 1875 mainlanders were appointed by the Collector and sent out as Amins to replace the Raja's Kariyakars and gumasthans. Men of the right stamp however would not take up the posts although the pay was Rs. 35 per mensem, and the men who were sent out proved as corrupt and incompetent as their predecessors. At the very next inspection in 1877 Mr. Winterbotham found it necessary to recommend the recall of all of them. He condemned the system of appointing mainlanders at all and proposed that competent islanders should be appointed as Amins on a salary of Rs. 25, assisted by mainlanders as gumasthans. This change was effected immediately and islanders have ever since been appointed as Amins. With the spread of education it has been found possible to secure islanders also sufficiently qualified for the post of gumasthan. These posts are not at present treated as hereditary. The Amin is almost always selected from among the Karanavars.

There is thus now on each island an Amin, with a gumasthan to assist him in his clerical work. The Amin has jurisdiction in petty civil and criminal cases. More important cases, and appeals from the Amin's decisions, lie within the jurisdiction of the Collector of Malabar who delegates his powers to the Headquarters Deputy Collector or to the officer annually deputed to inspect the islands. There is no appeal from their decisions to the Collector but revision petitions are entertained upon good cause being shown. Appeals lie to the High Court under the provisions of Regulation I of 1912.

Regulation I of 1912.

By this Regulation, passed on 22nd January 1912, Island law and procedure has been to some extent legalised and codified for the Malabar islands. Section 3 declares that the only enactments in force on the Malabar Islands are the Madras State Prisoners' Regulation (II of 1819), the State Prisoners' Act (XXXIV of 1850 and III of 1858), the Scheduled Districts Act (XIV of 1874) and the Regulation itself, thus removing any doubt that may have existed as to the applicability to the Malabar Islands of enactments declared to be in force on the South Kanara Islands.

The Reforms.

Upon the introduction of the Montagu Chelmsford Reforms both the groups were declared "Backward" tracts (Notification of the Governor-General, dated 3rd January 1921) and were excluded from the operations of the Legislative Councils. By the same notification the Governor is authorised to direct that any act of the local legislature shall not apply to the islands or shall apply subject to such exceptions or modifications as the Governor may think fit. No notification has yet (1922) been issued. Until one is issued, all enactments applicable to the whole Presidency, passed subsequent to the passing of the Government of India Act, will apply to both groups.

Placed in charge of Headquarters Deputy Collector.

In 1891 when inspections were not carried out annually the Malabar Islands were placed in charge of the Headquarters Deputy Collector. He has power to entertain all cases outside the jurisdiction of the Amins and to hear appeals from their decisions. The appeal time was originally fixed at six months. When inspections became annual, at any rate in theory, the practice grew up of allowing cases and appeals filed before the Collector or Deputy Collector to lie over until the yearly inspection took place so as to admit of their disposal on the islands themselves. As a means to the same end the monsoon months were excluded in reckoning the six months appeal time on the Amindivis. The same rule has been adopted for the Malabar islands also under Regulation I (Section 17). The Deputy Collector's powers have thus become merely nominal except in years when no inspection takes place.

Appeal time

Annual scrutiny of accounts.

Besides the annual inspection of the islands, a yearly scrutiny of the accounts is held in April or May. The Amins of the Malabar Islands attend at Calicut with their accounts and collections which are checked by the Island Department of the Collector's office. The Monegar of the South Kanara islands similarly attends the Collector's office at Mangalore for the check of his accounts and collections and he is further required to remain at Mangalore during the fair weather months to assist in receiving and paying for the shipments of coir. After a short period of leave which is then allowed him, he returns to Ameni before the monsoon bursts.

Inspections by two officers.

Inspections of both groups are made so far as possible annually by a Covenanted Civilian. The Collector of Malabar usually takes the opportunity to pay a short visit to one or two of the islands. Up to 1908 it was the practice to depute two officers on this inspection duty, one from South Kanara and one from Malabar. In 1909 one officer was deputed to inspect all the islands, the main reason for the change being in the first instance that Government wished the proposal to transfer the South Kanara islands to Malabar carefully explained to them by a Malabar official. The new arrangement was found to be not only economical, as one officer can do the work in very little longer time than it previously took each of the officers deputed, while the R.I.M. Steamer is required only to take the officer out to the northernmost island and meet him again at one of the southern islands to which he can work his way in island craft, but also more efficient in that the Malabar officer and his Malabar staff are in closer touch with the Amindivi people and are more easily and directly able to dispose of the work in Malayalam than the party sent from the South Kanara district could be, working as they had to do through interpreters. This arrangement is to be continued experimentally for a few years before it is finally decided whether or not to adopt it permanently.

G.O. No. 2662, Rev., 13th Aug. 1910.

By one officer for the whole group.

Medical Aid.

A dispensary was established at Ameni in 1874 in charge of a Hospital Assistant. In 1875 a midwife was attached to the institution. Originally the Hospital Assistant visited the other islands of the South Kanara group only occasionally. In 1881 it was ordered that he should visit each island once a year with the Monegar when the latter went on tour, and this is now regularly done. In addition he visits any island of the group upon the outbreak of cholera or any other epidemic. The Sub-Assistant Surgeon, as he is now styled, during these visits carries out vaccination on the outlying islands.

Epidemics of cholera have been common and, till the establishment of a Medical Officer at Ameni, carried off a large number of victims. The chief diseases treated at the dispensary are diseases of the stomach and bowels, worms, diseases of the skin, rheumatism and eye diseases. Ophthalmia and other eye diseases are, however, less common than formerly as a result probably of skilled treatment and advice being now available.

Although there has been a midwife attached to the dispensary since 1875, with short breaks, the people remain very ignorant and prejudiced, and avail themselves of her services but seldom. The methods of their own midwives are crude beyond belief and infantile mortality is in consequence very high.

There is no resident Medical Officer on the Malabar group. A dispensary in charge of a Hospital Assistant was established on Minicoy in 1891, but in 1901 it was transferred to Androth as the work being done was negligible owing mainly to the utter indifference of the islanders to modern medical treatment. The dispensary, after working at Androth for four years, was finally closed for the same reason in 1905. Subsequently a Sub-Assistant Surgeon has always been attached to the inspecting officer's staff and in addition to attending to the health of the inspecting party he treats the sick upon each island visited, carries out vaccination as far as possible, and looks to measures of sanitation and health. But this is all the medical aid available to the Malabar islands. All diseases are in consequence far more common than on the South Kanara islands, while epidemics of cholera levy a severe toll upon the inhabitants. The people have now come to see the advantages of proper medical and surgical treatment and are greatly desirous to have medical officers resident on the islands.

The Robinson Poor Fund. In 1844, Sir W. (then Mr.) Robinson was instrumental in salving a larger portion of the cargo of the *Ceylon* wrecked upon Cheriapani Reef. Government granted him a reward of Rs. 4,000 which he generously devoted to founding a Poor Fund for the benefit of the poor on the Amindivi islands. The fund now amounts to over Rs. 9,000 invested in Government Securities. The interest is devoted to the maintenance of deserving poor upon the South Kanara islands. There are usually from 10 to 12 persons on the Fund, some receiving relief at full and others at half rates.

The full rates are, for each recipient per annum, 4 muras 14½ seers of rice, 4½ yards of cloth, 24 lb. salt, 1 lb. tobacco and four annas' worth of condiments.

Education. Koran classes for both boys and girls appear to have been held on all the islands in connexion with the mosques from time immemorial. All children under a certain age attend these schools most regularly, but the instruction imparted goes no further than to enable the children to read Koran in Arabic characters and to recite large portions of it by heart. They are totally ignorant of the meaning of what they are reading or reciting. In the earlier years of British administration it was thought that the people were too backward to realise the value of education and it was not until 1885 that attempts to start a school on Ameni were made. In that year an islander was sent to the mainland and trained as a schoolmaster, the proposal being that he should, on his return, work in the mosque school under the Mukri. This he did, but after a little time the Mukri died and the teacher set up a small school independently of any mosque school, himself instructing the boys in the Koran. The result, ten years later, was found to be that the instruction given was little better than that imparted by the Koran schools as the teacher in addition to teaching the Koran imparted only a smattering of Malayalam to a few of the boys. By 1897 even this had ceased. Proposals to educate the islanders in Kanarese occupied the field for the next few years but fortunately were never carried out. In 1905 a trained teacher from the Local Board Panchama School, Kasaragode, was sent to Ameni and since then progress in education has been fairly steady. The school started with about 20 boys on the rolls. It has now over 80 and an assistant master has been appointed. Reading and writing in Malayalam, and arithmetic, are taught up to the fourth standard and also a little History and Geography.

Malabar islands.

Educational progress on the Malabar islands has been very similar. A school was started on Kalpeni in some year prior to 1884. A school on Kavarathi was started in 1884, and on Agathi somewhat later. Between 1890 and 1893 a small school existed on Minicoy. In 1891 a school was started on Androth. The attendance, however, at none of the schools much exceeded 20 and often fell below 10 and the instruction imparted was elementary. Since 1905 the schools have worked rather more systematically, though it can hardly be said that there is yet any widespread desire among the islanders for education, and it requires constant pressure on the part of inspecting officers to keep the attendance in the schools even moderately good. The schools are inspected by the inspecting officer. Results grants were formerly paid to the masters according to the passes obtained, for each pass in the Infant standard Re. 1, in I standard Rs. 2, in II standard Rs. 3, in III standard Rs. 4, in V standard Rs. 5. The masters on both groups in 1922 were placed upon a graded time-scale of pay (Rs. 20--1--30, and Rs. 25--1--50 for elementary and higher elementary grade teachers respectively) and results grants were abolished. The Agathi school, teaching up to the III standard had in 1920, 25 children on the rolls, the Kavarathi schcol teaching up to V standard 32, and the Kalpeni school teaching up to IV standard 81. The Androth school was temporarily closed for want of a teacher.

Revenue.

There is no system of Land Revenue upon any of the islands. The chief sources of revenue on the Laccadives proper excluding Minicoy, are now the coir monopoly, rents of Pandaram lands, rents of the uninhabited islands, Tinnakara, Bangaram and Suheli, and magisterial fines. There were also previously certain minor monopolies which have now been abandoned.

The coir monopoly.

Coir is a monopoly on all the islands except Minicoy. The monopoly was first introduced in 1765 by Bommaly Raja who used the power and wealth he had acquired through the exertions of his Vizier, Kunhi Pakki, to establish a monopoly of purchase over the principal products of the islands. The market value of coir was then between Rs. 60 and Rs. 70 per candy and the price paid to the islanders was fixed at Rs. 30—35 per candy, paid in rice at a commutation price of Rs. 2¼ per robbin, but the actual price paid was reduced to about Rs. 23½ per candy by deduction of an import duty upon the coir itself at Cannanore, of an export duty upon the rice supplied in payment, and of further small sums on account of Nazzeranas and petty expenses. This gave a profit of Rs. 40—50 per candy and it is estimated that the monopoly produced in the early years a revenue to the Raja of between Rs. 65,000 and Rs. 75,000 which must have been very largely increased shortly afterwards when the price of rice began to fall. So strict and harsh was the enforcement of the monopoly that in 1784 it gave rise to the revolt of the northern islands, which secured much easier terms from Tippu. From this date onward to the present time the monopoly has been worked rather differently in the two groups and its history in each will be traced separately.

Robinson II, pp. 33 38.

Immense profits in early years.

Subsequent history.

In the early years of British rule on the South Kanara islands the coir was all paid for at a uniform rate of Rs. 25 per candy, one-fourth being paid in cash and three-fourths in rice at a commutation price of Rs. 2 per muda. It is unknown how or when the practice of paying a portion of the price in cash was first introduced. It is found firmly established in 1820. The monopoly was worked without any of the harshness and oppression which characterised the same system upon the Cannanore islands and the people early realised the advantages they derived from it. A uniform classification, however, tended to encourage the production of poor coir and in 1820 a second class paid for at Rs. 20 and subsequently even a third class at Rs. 17-8-0 was evolved, without definite orders, by the Collector's establishment. This led to complaints from the islanders of unfairness and delay in sorting, and to meet them it was ordered in 1837, on the recommendation of a panchayat of islanders and merchants, that there should in future be no separation into classes or examination as to quality, but that a

Robinson I, pp. 43-53.

On the South Kanara islands.

fixed proportion of all the coir should be paid for as first, second and third class. It was found that the result of the previous classification had been to place on the average 66 per cent in the first class, 23 per cent in the second class and 11 per cent in the third and the following proportions were fixed:— No sorting into classes.

Ameni and Kadamat—

70 per cent first class at Rs. 21-14-0 per candy.
20 per cent second class at Rs. 17-8-0 per candy.
10 per cent third class at Rs. 13-2-0 per candy.

Kiltan and Chetlat—

80 per cent first class.
15 per cent second class.
5 per cent third class.

One-fourth of the price was still paid in cash and three-fourths in rice.

This system worked at first most satisfactorily. It put a stop to the endless complaints brought by the islanders against the sorting establishment and it relieved the Collector's office of all the trouble of classifying the coir, while the islanders for their part refrained from taking advantage of it to produce inferior coir.

Until 1826, the Bombay and Bengal Governments took all the coir received at Mangalore at Rs. 65 per candy which left a good margin of profit upon the transactions. After that year, however the demand and with it the prices for coir rapidly fell, and the prices were not infrequently below the actual prices paid to the islanders. This unsatisfactory condition of things was remedied to some extent by a corresponding fall in the price of rice. In 1846 Sir W. Robinson calculated that with rice as it then was at 25 per cent below the commutation rate of Rs. 2 per muda, Government saved 18¾ per cent of the price paid, while a charge of ½ maund of coir per muda of rice supplied, levied as a Sea Customs duty and placed in arrear against each boat and deducted the next year before any coir was paid for, reduced the price paid by another 18¾ per cent, making a total saving of 37 per cent in all; in other words instead of paying Rs. 21-14-0 per candy for first-class coir Government were only paying Rs. 14-0-0. In spite of this, however, Sir W. Robinson calculated that the net profit for the preceding 15 years was only Rs. 3,741 excluding the Rs. 5,250 paid to the Bibi of Cannanore, while if that was included in the disbursements there had been an actual surplus only in two years, 1836 and 1837. The profits.

Coir continued to fall in value and the price of rice steadily rose, yet the financial position as reviewed at each inspection remained for many years wonderfully satisfactory, and

prognostications of the speedy bankruptcy of the island administration were unfulfilled. In 1866 the transactions for the years since Sir W. Robinson's visit showed a net average revenue of Rs. 9,271 per annum. In 1869 this average annual profit had risen to Rs. 11,508. In 1873 it had fallen for the previous four years to Rs. 7,437 but had risen again in 1880 to Rs. 8,818, although owing to a rise in prices the islanders were being paid at the equivalent of Rs. 30 per candy. By
Are replaced by an annual loss.
1891 the average profit had fallen to Rs. 2,693. In 1893 it was only Rs. 1,145 and by 1895 an adverse balance of Rs. 5,465 had accumulated.

This result had been foretold by various inspecting officers, notably by Sir W. Robinson so early as 1846 and by Sir G. Stokes in 1873 on the economic ground that the price of
G.O. No. 387, Rev., 26th March 1874.
coconuts must tend to fall while the price of rice, a food stuff, must tend to rise. The conclusions were correct but there was an additional reason other than the rise and fall of prices that helped to cause the disappearance of the monopoly profits. This was in fact the laziness of the people themselves. Being paid for the greater portion of the coir at first-
The reason.
class rates, on a fixed proportion of the output, whether it was really first-class or not, they ceased to exert themselves to produce first-class coir which not only takes far longer to manufacture but bulks smaller and is lighter than the inferior kinds. The natural result was that the prices fetched by Ameni coir in the market began steadily to decline. The total output also became yearly smaller, and from both these causes the revenue steadily shrank until as stated above in 1895 there was a large deficit.

It had been clearly seen for some years previously that energetic steps would have to be taken to improve the class of coir and increase the outturn if the islands were to continue
G.O. No. 1428, 9th September 1870.
to pay their way. Even so far back as 1869 Mr. H. S. Thomas had proposed to encourage the production of good coir by allowing the islanders a proportion (15 per cent) of the enhanced prices that would be obtained. The Board of Revenue preferred to give the islanders a fixed 25 per cent of the net profit in each year but Mr. Thomas objected that this would make the islanders' profits depend not upon their own
G.O. No. 387, 26th March 1874.
industry but on economies in the administration. By 1873 it was seen that the enhanced prices were due not to improvements in manufacture but to a rise in the price of coir and the proposal was dropped. In 1873 Mr. Stokes foresaw the necessity of keeping the output at a figure sufficient to defray the cost of the administration and on his recommendation a fine was imposed if less than 674 candies were exported. In

1891 Messrs. Morgan & Sons offered, if given a monopoly, to set up coir-spinning machinery on the islands and attempt by improved modern methods to improve both the quality and the quantity of island coir. Government refused to grant the monopoly on the ground that the proposal would too entirely upset economic conditions on the islands and interfere too greatly with the islanders' principal means of livelihood. On Mr. Slight's report in 1894 Government sanctioned the re-introduction of the system of classification abandoned in 1837 but there was some delay in actually making the change. Mr. Couchman who visited the islands in 1895 selected samples of what should be considered first, second and third-class coir. Sealed samples were left on each island as a standard; a set was deposited in the Collector's office at Mangalore, and the new classification and new prices were to have been introduced with effect from 1896. The orders of Government however, as to prices had been misunderstood and the scheme did not come into force until 1898. All coir equal to or better than Mr. Couchman's second-class sample was treated as first class and paid for at Rs. 21-14-0 per candy all equal to or better than his third sample as second-class at Rs. 17-8-0, all below that as third class at Rs. 13-2-0, one-fouth of the price being paid as before in cash and three-fourths in rice. In addition, in order to encourage the manufacture of first-class coir and to give the producer a share in the profits, 25 per cent of the actual price realized in the market for first-class coir was to be added to the price paid for it. This, however, appears never to have been done. The classification was carried out by a special staff at Mangalore under the supervision of the Port Officer.

G.O. No. 310, Rev., 30th March 1892.

G.O. No. 576, 8th August 1894.

Classification reintroduced.

G.O. No. 104, 10th January 1896.

One and a half maunds of salt were supplied free of tax for every candy of coir. This privilege of importing salt free was first granted in 1866 when 1 maund was allowed free for every candy of coir. It was then a valuable concession and is calculated to have cost Government between Rs. 700 and Rs. 800 per annum. With the reduction in the salt tax the value of the privilege was reduced, yet it was still prized and the Malabar islanders who did not participate, frequently petitioned to have the concession extended to them.

Duty free salt.

The reintroduction of classification had at once some effect. In 1896 it was found that almost all the coir imported was only equal to Mr. Couchman's third-class sample. There was a natural decrease at first in the quantity produced but under the efforts of successive Inspecting Officers and the Monegar the quality steadily improved up to a point. The amount of first-class coir never, however, again approached

Improvement in coir.

the percentage fixed in 1837. It is legitimate perhaps to suppose that the classification then was not so strict and that much of the so-called first-class coir was only equal to the present second-class. On the other hand it has to be remembered that the increased price given for better class coir did not reach the actual spinners as they were still paid by the boat owners in rice at the old mamul rates which prevailed before the system of classification was introduced, and the system therefore had only an indirect effect through the boat owners upon the spinners. In 1891 the average price obtained by Government for the coir was Rs. 38-15-0 but already by 1901 it had improved to Rs. 49-8-0.

On the Malabar islands.

On the Malabar islands the history of the monopoly was rather different. Even after the revolt of the northern islands the system continued to be worked on the southern group with as much rigour as before. But with the death of Tippu there was no longer any rival to the Cannanore family upon whose protection the southern islanders could throw themselves, and the Bombay Government, although repeatedly appealed to and although they at first ordered the immediate surrender of the monopoly, found it impossible as already explained, to abolish the system. By 1869 a state of anarchy had been reached and it was only the attachment of the islands by Government in 1875 with the consequent amelioration of the abuses in the system that prevented the islands from completely renouncing their allegiance to the Raja.

Payments in rice.

Robinson II, p. 34.

Logan's report, 1869.

The system of payment partly in cash and partly in rice did not prevail at first on the Malabar islands. Up to 1826 the monopoly price had been Rs. 30 per candy paid entirely in rice at Rs. 2¼ per muda. Deducting the 20 per cent import duty at Cannanore upon the coir and on the islands upon the rice, this gave the islanders a clear 10⅔ mudas of rice. In that year however the price of coir fell greatly and the price paid to the islanders was correspondingly reduced to 5¾ mudas; as the cost of production was calculated to be 5⅓ mudas, the margin of profit to the islanders can have been almost nothing and it is little wonder that the monopoly came to be practically in abeyance. In consequence the Raja was forced in 1865 to raise the price to Rs. 20 and in 1869 he was prepared to pay Rs. 25. The Collector sought to induce him to raise it to Rs. 30, but he represented that he could not do so without serious loss although Government was at the time paying the equivalent of Rs. 35 for Amindivi coir and still realising a profit. Government determined in 1871 that, in view of the abuses of the system which, as then worked, was benefitting neither the Raja nor the islanders, they could not assist him to enforce the monopoly. Nor could it be expected that he would be able unaided to do so himself. They advised him to abolish it of his own accord, and levy the revenue in some less objectionable way. On the occasion of the next visit to the islands in 1873 (by Mr. Spedding) it was found that the Raja had taken no action whatever, affairs on the islands had grown steadily worse and there were besides large arrears of peshkash accumulating against the Raja which, in the absence of any receipts from the monopoly, he was unable to pay off. Partly to clear these arrears, but more particularly in order to introduce a better revenue system, Government attached the islands in 1875. Between 1874 and 1877 Mr. Logan, the Collector of Malabar, who had himself visited the islands in 1869, submitted different schemes for raising a revenue. His proposals, which entailed the abolition of the monopoly, were not accepted, but under the orders of the Board of Revenue (B.P. No. 490, dated 18th February 1876) and for reasons which Mr. Logan had himself set out in his report of 1869, the prices paid were assimilated in 1876 to those paid on the South Kanara islands, namely, Rs. 21-14-0 per candy for first class, Rs. 17-8-0 for second class and Rs. 13-2-0 for third-class coir, three-fourths of the price as on the South Kanara islands was to be paid for in rice and one-fourth in cash but no salt was issued free of tax. Thus the new system on the Malabar islands was deliberately copied from that prevailing on the northern islands.

G.O. No. 405, Pol., 20th Dec. 1871.

South Kanara system adopted.

There was, however, some misunderstanding at first. It was thought that the whole price was to be paid in money, and in order to effect this a commutation rate was fixed each year at the price of rice prevailing in the market at the time. This commutation rate remained fixed during the coir season whether the market price of rice rose or fell. The mistake was rectified by Mr. Logan who for convenience rounded off the annas in the South Kanara prices and fixed the Malabar prices in whole rupees at Rs. 22 for first class, Rs. 18 for second and Rs. 14 for third. But a further modification was also made which does not seem to have been contemplated in the first instance and which did not prevail as regards the South Kanara islands. At the price of rice prevailing in 1877 it was found that the amount of rice and money paid was in round figures for first-class coir 4 sacks of rice and Rs. 6, for second class 3½ sacks and Rs. 4 and for third class 2½ sacks and Rs. 3. These rates were introduced from 1st January 1878. Until 1905 the value of the fixed quantity of rice was calculated and the whole price of the coir was paid in money. In that year, on the representation of the islanders

With a difference.

G.O. No 7, Pol., 23rd Feb. 1880.

G.O. No. 592, Pol., 9th Oct. 1906.

it was agreed that they should be paid the fixed quantity of rice in rice without commutation into money, and it was arranged that the rice should be delivered to them by the Port officer at Mangalore although the sorting of the coir was still done by the Port officer at Calicut. This arrangement was made to suit the convenience of the islanders who almost invariably had to go as far north as Mangalore before proceeding on their return journey to the islands and who preferred the South Kanara to the Malabar rice. The sorting continued to be carried out at Calicut until 1913 when it was transferred to Mangalore.

Difficulty of maintaining the output.

G.O. No. 348, Pol., 8th June 1905.

G.O. No. 315, Pol., 1st July 1907.

As on the South Kanara islands, it was only by constant attention that the annual output of coir, in spite of the liberal rates which the islanders now received, was kept up to the average. The matter engaged the attention of every Inspecting Officer for many years and various proposals were made to secure a sufficient outturn. In 1904 Mr. Cotton recommended, and Mr. Pinhey, the Collector, supported the proposal, that a minimum output of 1,500 candies estimated to produce a revenue of Rs. 5,000, should be fixed and that boat owners should be fined for any deficiency, but Government did not agree to this, pointing out that the fines would certainly not fall upon the real defaulters. In 1906 the output had declined still further, showing a drop of 25 per cent from the figures of even four years before. When questioned by Mr. Thomas, who visited the islands in that year, the people attributed the fall to bad seasons for coconuts, increased strictness in sorting the coir and to the boat owners dishonestly taking inferior rice from the merchants and sharing with them the difference, but the truth appears to have been that about that time the price of coconuts and copra rose enormously, and the people, who found they could realise high prices for these new commodities and thereby obtain sufficient money to support themselves with but little labour, naturally declined to undertake the more laborious task of manufacturing coir merely to provide a revenue for Government. As a contributory cause it may be mentioned that the women upon whom the whole labour falls, had no inducement to increase their toil because they knew that whatever was obtained over and above that necessary to provide for the bare needs of the family would only be squandered by their husbands while the boats were on the coast. Moreover, the money portion of the price was appropriated by the boat owners on account of freightage and the rice was paid to the shippers at the same mamul rates which prevailed before the introduction of the sorting system.

G.O. No. 96, 20th Feb. 1909.

G.O. No. 1882, 14th July 1909.

Further enquiries were instituted during the visits of 1907 and 1908 as to the possibility of introducing some other means of raising a revenue for the Malabar islands, and, although it was decided that no change was desirable, the islanders were warned that if the revenue from the coir monopoly fell some change would have to be made. The islanders are keenly alive to the benefits they derive from the monopoly and the warning had the desired effect.

An unstable source of income.

It will be seen, however, that the coir monopoly is not a satisfactory source of revenue. The amount it may produce depends upon three constantly changing factors: the amount of coir produced by the islanders, its market price, and the market price of rice, and can never be forecasted. Nor is there any guarantee that it will in any year be sufficient to meet the expenses of the administration. For these reasons proposals have been made from time to time for its abolition on both groups. So long ago as 1835 Mr. Cotton had recommended a change of system on the northern group but the proposal was strongly opposed by the islanders themselves and it came early to be recognised that as enforced by the Hon. Company and afterwards by Government the monopoly was not only not oppressive but actually highly beneficial to the people. In 1846 Sir W. Robinson after his inspection put forward some forcible arguments in favour of maintaining the monopoly. He pointed out that the tax imposed by it was extremely light, representing not more than one-sixth of the produce of a tree, and was paid indirectly by the barter of surplus produce for rice, while Government participated directly and by an automatic process in any failure of crop. His opinion was that if left to dispose of the coir themselves, the people would experience great difficulty in finding a market and would find it quite impossible to watch the market and dispose of their coir to the best advantage. He considered various alternatives: a system of export or import duties, which he rejected as liable to lead to illicit trade: some scheme of assessment levied on trees, which seemed to him impossible, as each man's trees were scattered, and far too complicated to be worked with the existing staff: or some system of islandwar assessment paid by one responsible person and levied by him from individuals, which he also rejected as almost certain to lead to oppression and injustice. In 1873 Mr. (now Sir) G. Stokes again proposed the abolition of the monopoly, but his recommendation was not accepted and the opinion of all Inspecting Officers for the South Kanara islands since that date has been strongly in favour of a continuance of the monopoly.

Its abolition proposed for the Amindivis.

Robinson I, p. 47.

Sir W. Robinson contra.

Subsequent opinions. G.O. No. 387 26th Mar. 1874.

Sir W. Robinson proposes its abolition on the Malabar islands.

The fact that on the Malabar islands the monopoly was enforced by the Raja entirely altered its effect upon the people. In 1847 Sir W. Robinson was compelled to argue as strongly for its abolition on these islands as he had the year before urged its retention on the Amindivi islands while the people themselves never ceased to cry out against its iniquities until the islands were finally attached in 1875. As already stated the main object of the attachment was to introduce some other system and it was decided that the islands, should not be restored until some other means of raising the revenue had been found, as even from his own point of view the Raja could hardly be expected to remain content with the uncertain proceeds of the monopoly and could not afford to balance the lean years with the fat as Government might do.

Mr. Logan's earliest schemes.

G.O. No. 405, Pol., 20th Dec. 1871.

Mr. Logan, who as Special Assistant Collector visited the islands in 1869, reported strongly against the monopoly and recommended the substitution of either a poll tax or a land tax.* Mr. Macgregor, the then Collector of Malabar, objected to both proposals, to the first on the score that it would be impossible to check abuses, and to the second on the grounds that it would entail the introduction of a regular survey and settlement and the consequent raising of difficult questions of ownership, and that it was quite unworkable with the existing establishment. In the alternative he suggested a moderate export duty, either on coir only, or else, if necessary, on all produce of the coconut and on all other monopoly products. Government, while acquiescing in the necessity of abolishing the monopoly, found legal objections to the Collector's proposal and suggested that the Raja might be induced to accept a fixed annual payment in coir which might be revised every ten years, in lieu of the monopoly. When the question next came up, on the inspection of the islands by Mr. Spedding in 1873, Mr. Logan was Collector of Malabar. It had been found impossible to persuade the Raja to accept the Government's proposal and in advising upon the next step to be taken Mr. Logan represented the difficulty of distributing among the people the fixed amount to be paid to the Raja. He recommended Mr. Macgregor's scheme for imposing an export duty on coir and other products of the coconut. He calculated the "jamma" payable by the Raja on Cannanore, the four Malabar islands and Minicoy to be Rs. 9,750 (Rs. 15,000 peshkash less Rs. 5,250 payable for the South Kanara islands) and as it had

G.O. No. 107, Pol., 17th Feb. 1875.

Monopoly to be replaced by an export duty.

* Mr. Logan, however, explained subsequently that his report was misunderstood and that he had never any intention of recommending a land tax (vide his letter No. 41, dated 15th May 1873, printed in G.O. No. 107, Pol., dated 17th February 1875).

been agreed between the Bibi and the Malabar Commissioners in 1793 that the jamma should be "a moiety of whatever is or shall be ascertained to be the produce of her country," it followed that the total revenue to be raised was Rs. 19,500. Rs. 3,800 being the sum already fixed as the jamma for Cannanore, Rs. 7,600 would be raised for the Cannanore lands and the balance Rs. 11,900 would be the amount to be levied upon the Malabar Laccadives and Minicoy. Assuming that Government would impose a tax of one-sixth of all coconut produce, Mr. Logan calculated that the four northern Malabar islands would contribute Rs. 9,500, while the balance of Rs. 2,400 would be levied upon Minicoy. The Raja's revenue from the islands would then be his "moiety" Rs. 9,750, together with the rents of his private land on the islands.

Mr. Logan's first proposal was that the tax should be levied in kind at the port of import. Subsequently in his letter No. 319, dated 25th December 1876, he modified this and advised payment in cash as he feared Government would be unable to sell to advantage the small quantities of the different commodities which they would receive under the other proposal. He added calculations to show that assuming that the islanders should pay a tax of Rs. 1-8-0 per head, equal to the incidence of land assessment per head in the Presidency, a tax of 8 per cent on the total coconut exports would yield the required amount from the Malabar Laccadives, while there would be no necessity to extend the scheme to Minicoy which had yielded an income of Rs. 7,000. No orders were passed on either proposal till 2nd July 1877 and by that time Government had altered their opinion as to the advisability of abolishing the monopoly. In their order No. 416 of that date they decided that further experience must be gained before any final orders could be issued and they remained of opinion that the enforcement of any export duty at the port of import would be illegal. Mr. Logan, however, was so impressed with the urgent necessity for some change that he brought the matter up again before the inspection of 1877, but Government telegraphed their refusal. Again in his Administration Report for fasli 1286-87 (vide his letter No. 46, dated 10th March 1879) he urged that he might be allowed to introduce his system at least tentatively on Androth, with the further modification that the duty should be levied on the island itself. Government gave way so far as to permit the proposed experiment and asked Mr. Logan to report the particulars of his scheme, but at the same time declared that the total abolition of the monopoly was a measure to which they had always been opposed. Before

G.O. No. 416, Pol., 2nd July 1877.

G.O. No. 662, 28th Nov. 1877.

G.O. No. 721, dated 23rd Feb. 1880.

G.O. No. 569, 14th Dec. 1881.

proceeding on leave Mr. Logan drew up a note showing the proposed arrangements for an export duty to be introduced as an experiment upon Androth on his return. He calculated that out of the total of Rs. 11,900 to be levied upon all the Laccadives the share of Androth would be Rs. 2,975 and, assuming that this should be net revenue, added establishment and other charges which brought the total sum to be raised to Rs. 3,800. Deducting the rents (Rs. 1,003) of the Rāja's private land, which Mr. Logan now proposed to regard as part of the revenue, the balance actually leviable was Rs. 2,797. The total exports of coconut produce from Androth were valued at about Rs. 36,549 a duty of 7⅔ per cent upon which would produce the required revenue. Government however in reviewing the scheme reverted to their former opinion that "some arrangement under which a certain amount of coir would be received in kind and sold on behalf of Government would be more in accordance with principle in a rude society of the kind." The Inspecting Officer of that year (Mr. Underwood) was ordered to report on the suggestion but he had already sailed for the islands before the Government Order was issued. Under the circumstances the Board of Revenue (in Board's Proceedings No. 39, dated 6th January 1893) in their review of Mr. Underwood's report, approved of Mr. Logan's scheme and seemed to take for granted that it was being introduced. Mr. Logan however had not returned to Malabar and the new scheme was not put into force. His successor, Mr. Dalton directed Mr. Tate, the Inspecting Officer of 1884, to report upon both it and the Government's proposal. Mr. Tate found the people strongly opposed to any change, for the reason that under the monopoly system they had no trouble in disposing of their coir quickly and at a fixed price, while if they had to sell it themselves in open market they would probably be cheated by the merchants and would have to take any price that might be ruling at the time, as they could not afford to wait on the mainland for a rise, and thus might often have to accept prices far below a subsistence rate. He pointed out several practical difficulties in applying Mr. Logan's scheme and expressed himself opposed to any change. Mr. Dalton in his covering letter agreed that there was no advantage in altering the existing system and observed that its previous unpopularity among the islanders had been due solely to the malpractices rife in the Rāja's time, which under the management of Government officials had been completely removed. Government in their order expressed themselves convinced that the continuance of the monopoly system was desirable. Thus Malabar officials and

The proposal shelved.

G.O. No. 292, Pol., 4th May 1886.

Mr. Tate reports against abolition.

Government agree.

the islanders themselves came gradually to hold the same views upon the beneficial effects of the monopoly, when administered by Government, as the South Kanara officials, who had only seen it so administered, had entertained from the first. Even Mr. Logan, the strongest advocate of change, seems only to have urged it because he clearly realised that the monopoly could not be retained if the islands were again to be handed back to the Raja. It was the necessity for finding some alternative source of revenue as little open to abuse as possible, against the time when the attachment of the islands should cease, that had been ever present to his mind. He returned to Malabar at the end of 1884 and at once set about formulating a fresh scheme which he embodied in a letter to the Board. Mr. Logan urged that though the monopoly might suit the islanders and be workable so long as the islands were administered by Government, to whom temporary losses were immaterial, it must be a failure when worked by the Raja who could not afford to lose in bad years on the chance of being recouped in good ones, an inability on his part which must prove fatal to the fair and equitable administration of the monopoly. Mr. Logan's new proposal was nothing less than a land assessment to be paid in coir, based upon a complete survey and providing for 5 different classes of land, but skilfully combining also the provisions of the improving leases under which the Raja's private lands were held. Mr. Logan claimed that his new scheme was in fact the very arrangements approved by Government in 1881 "under which a certain amount of coir would be received in kind and sold for Government account" but it is hardly necessary to point out that Government then had objected to a regular land assessment and that their proposal of that date had been quite different. Government however agreed to the scheme and ordered that it should be carried into effect as early as possible. Mr. Logan himself was to visit the islands in March 1886 and introduce his scheme. But once more circumstances prevented the introduction of any change. No steamer could be obtained to take the Inspection party to the islands that year, and in 1887 only hurried visits could be paid to restore order on Minicoy. In 1888 Mr. Logan had left Malabar and his successor Mr. Winterbotham expressed himself opposed to any change, which would be particularly invidious just then, when Government were losing on the monopoly owing to a fall in the price of coir. He pointed out that if it was still supposed that a scheme was being matured which would enable the Cannanore family to resume the government, they were really as far from the goal as ever. He did not

G.O. No. 416, Pol., 2nd July 1877.

B.P. No. 472, 12th Feb. 1885.

Mr. Logan again urges abolition.

And proposes a land assessment.

G.O. No. 748, Pol., 28th Oct. 1885.

Frustrated by circumstances.

Letter No. 4057, R., 1 Nov. 1888.

Mr. Winterbotham opposes abolition.

believe that any system could be invented which the Raja, however good his intentions, could carry on, and he thought the best course was to tell him once and for all that he must give up his sovereignty and then to carry on the existing arrangements. This letter did not reach Government through the Board until March 1889 and they deferred passing orders on it until after Mr. Twigg's inspection of the islands in that year. Mr. Twigg's report confirmed Mr. Winterbotham in the views he had expressed, and Government concurred that any idea of abolishing the monopoly against the will of the islanders must for some time to come be abandoned.

And Government agree. G.O. No. 229, Pol., 11th May 1889.

The question reopened 1907.

The question was dropped from that time until in 1907 Mr. Knapp suggested that the Inspecting Officer of that year should make special enquiry, in view of the steady decrease in revenue, whether the islanders would not prefer to pay a tree-tax in place of the monopoly. Mr. Lancashire, the Inspecting Officer for 1907 accordingly investigated the whole system. As a result he formed the opinion that any change was most undesirable, giving as his main reason the fact that the islanders would be quite unable to watch the market and hold out for higher prices and would be entirely in the power of the merchants. He drew attention to the amount of coir that had to be held over by Government from one year to another in order to secure a good price. To take only the ten preceding years, in fasli 1308 nearly one-third, in fasli 1310 about half, in fasli 1311 one-third, in fasli 1315 one-fourth, and in fasli 1316 again one third had thus to be held over. The conclusions then arrived at were confirmed during the inspection of 1908 and it was pointed out in the report for that year that while the cost price of second-class coir was Rs. 39, the average highest selling price for ten years had been only Rs. 39-11-7 while the average lowest selling price was Rs. 34-14-0 and the lowest price accepted Rs. 30, or Rs. 9 less than Government was paying the islanders. It seemed almost certain that if left to trade for themselves the islanders would be forced to accept even lower prices. It was suggested that if an increase of revenue was considered absolutely necessary, an export tax of 5 per cent on the lines of Mr. Logan's proposal, levied at the port of import, might be imposed and would produce roughly about Rs. 8,000 but that the coir monopoly, which it was pointed out was really no tax at all, must in any eventuality be retained in the interests of the people. Government in their order on the report decided that no change was called for. The result, however, of the European war, coupled with the poor harvests in 1918 and 1919, was to raise the price of rice to an abnormal height

G.O. No. 96, Pol., 20th Feb. 1909.

Further reasons against abolition reported.

G.O. No. 1882, Pol., 14th July 1909

while the price of coir was not proportionately so much affected. In consequence, from 1916 onwards the monopoly resulted in very large deficits for both groups. Government decided to refrain from making any changes while conditions were so adverse for the islanders. In 1920 when prices had returned to a more normal level the whole question was once again examined by the Inspecting Officer. It was urged that in the interests of the islanders the monopoly must be retained but proposals were submitted for abolishing the classification, altering the method of payment to one purely in rice at the rate of 3½ thulams of coir per muda of rice, the payments in money and the free issue of salt being dropped altogether. To stimulate production it was also proposed that the monigar and amins should buy coir for rice on the islands direct from the spinners at a slightly higher rate of 4 thulams per muda. These proposals have been sanctioned and are now (1922) being introduced on all the islands, with the further modification that all the coir is being purchased on the islands themselves. It is hoped that this arrangement for taking over all the coir on the islands will relieve the poorer classes, at least so far as rice is concerned, from their oppressive dealings with the boat owners, and will also greatly stimulate production, as every twister can without difficulty or delay get rice on the island itself in return for her coir. Government have also under contemplation the possibility of raising some revenue from the islands from some other source.

The 1922 Scheme. G.O. No. 1321, Rev., 19th July 1922.

The Cannanore family appears to have had at first no private property on the islands. The Raja never at any time advanced any claims of overlordship over the lands in the occupation of the people and these lands or rather the trees upon them (for the idea of property in the land itself seems to be of recent growth) were always treated as the absolute property of the islanders. But about 100 years after the Cannanore Rajas came into the possession of the islands they began to assume the unoccupied lands on the inhabited islands and the entire area of the uninhabited islands. These lands, the private property of the Cannanore Pandaram or Government have come to be known as Pandaram lands in distinction from the people's private property.

Pandaram Rents.

Sir W. Robinson found the process of assumption still in progress in 1847 on the inhabited islands. The Pandaram claims were then only fully admitted in respect of the plantations and waste land on Androth and Kalpeni. Attempts were being made to assume the lands on Kavarathi and about 20 years before a strip 40 kols wide all along the shore had been summarily confiscated. This strip round

The Raja's claims only recent.

Robinson II, p. 82.

Pandarams on Kavarathi how acquired.

Robinson II, p. 70.

the shore constitutes what have since been known as the Chuttu Karaima lands. The Pandaram's claims to them were relinquished in 1870. In the years subsequent to 1847 every opportunity to secure land was availed of. Much was wrongfully declared escheat and cases are reported in which the Raja settled disputes as to property by himself appropriating it. In some such way may have been acquired the small blocks of Pandaram lands scattered among the private lands on Kavarathi and known as the "Nāttagạthu Kāraima." The present Idiyakkal Pandaram lands on Kavarathi were taken under management possibly about 1850 for debts due to the Pandaram and leased back to the owner, a member of the Idiyakkal family, but finally confiscated and rented to the highest bidder, although the profits of the management must have more than cleared the debt. A wall, the remains of which are still visible, was built across Kavarathi just south of the village and no islander was allowed to cross it into the southern portion, which is in consequence even now known as the Pandaram Pāk (forbidden ground). The land immediately south of the wall is known as the "Pādhi Pādhi." The plantations on it appear to have been made by the people themselves at a time when the Pandaram lands were left in their management, a fixed rental only being demanded. Subsequently when the Pandaram lands were resumed, the people were allowed to retain these plantations, the Pandaram taking half the produce as rent, and hence their name. The remainder of the Pandaram Pāk was waste at the date of Sir W. Robinson's visit, with the exception of five plantations made by the Raja's Kariyakars, whose names two of them now bear (Ali Mussa Valappu and Hussein Kariyakar Valappu).

By 1869 the Pandaram's claims to these lands seem to have become fully established, for Mr. Logan in his report for that year does not mention any rival claims being put forward. In the years of anarchy that followed it is remarkable to find that the Pandaram lands were nearly always respected and that few attempts to encroach upon or appropriate them were made.

Nothing is known as to the history of the Pandaram lands other than those mentioned above.

Disposal of Government trees on Amindivis.

On the South Kanara islands Government from the commencement adopted the very liberal policy of distributing the Pandaram trees and such other trees as have subsequently by escheat come into their possession, among poor and deserving islanders. The undistributed balance is leased out by the monigar annually but, is always available for distribution. Until recently the monigar was also required to plant sufficient young trees each year to ensure a supply for future distributions, but Government have now ordered that new planting should be stopped and in a few years all the trees available will either have been distributed or will have gone out of bearing.

On the Malabar islands, the Pandaram lands, being the private property of the Rajas, had to be retained and managed to the best possible advantage. Beyond plucking the nuts more or less irregularly, the Kariyakars had paid little attention to these properties and had entirely neglected replanting so that when the islands came under attachment the number of trees had seriously diminished compared with the number reported by Sir W. Robinson. Mr. Logan turned his attention to this branch of the administration. Although of opinion that the waste lands could not be the private property of the Raja, as the idea of property in land was quite unknown on the islands, he saw clearly that it would be impossible to leave them ownerless for any one who pleased to grab and he decided that the only alternative was to view them as the "crown property" of the Arakal family and to lease them out as such. His distinction between private and crown property may in the circumstances seem somewhat fine, but his conclusion was eminently wise. In consultation with Mr. Winterbotham who visited the islands in that year (1878) a scheme for granting the lands on improving leases or cowles was drawn up. It necessitated in the first instance a survey of all the Pandaram lands on the islands and the division of them into suitable plots. Then an inspection had to be made of each plot and the number of trees in the different stages of growth, phalam (bearing), aphalam (out of bearing), maram (young tree not yet in full bearing), kili (plant), thei (seedling), had to be recorded. A form of lease was drawn up which provided for the immediate payment of assessment upon all bearing trees and for necessary changes in assessment each year as the young trees, as ascertained at the inspection, came into bearing (paragraph 1 (*a*), (*b*), (*c*) of lease). No assessment was to be paid until after a fixed term of years upon trees planted by the lessee himself subsequent to the grant and, it was provided that under the orders of the Collector future paimashes might be made at intervals or after the destruction of trees by any serious calamity, and the assessment enhanced or lowered accordingly. The lessee was secured in possession for 40 years, subject to regular payment of assessment but could claim no compensation for improvements, such as buildings. It is evident

G.O. No. 72, Pol., 23rd Feb. 1880.

Disposal of Pandaram lands on the Malabar islands.

Improving leases.

however that from the first it was intended that the leases should run in perpetuity, although to meet exceptional circumstances this saving clause was entered. In 1883 the Board and Government seem to have contemplated the ultimate establishment through the leases of a property in land, in the cowle plots themselves first, to be extended afterwards to the whole area of the islands. It is interesting to note that time has as yet failed to induce much sense of possession over the land in even the cowle plots.

Survey of Pandaram property.

The Inspecting Officers of the years immediately following the introduction of the cowles, were chiefly occupied in the laborious task of surveying and paimashing the Pandaram property preliminary to leasing it out to the islanders. It was impossible to do more than a portion at each visit. A commencement was made by Mr. Winterbotham in 1878. Something more was done by Mr. V. A. Brodie in 1880. The work was carried on by Mr. Underwood in 1882 and finally completed by Mr. Tate in 1884. Minor alterations were introduced into the conditions of the lease by each officer, and as it was thought desirable that all leases should be on uniform terms the matter was reported to Government and after some discussion an amended form was finally approved in 1885. The conditions remained practically the same but the power to surrender at one year's notice was added.

G.O. No. 748, Pol., 28th Oct. 1885.

Government ordered the abolition of the sharing system on the Pādhi Pādhi lands in 1873, but their instructions were misunderstood and it was not until 1891 that the leases of these lands were assimilated to the other Pandaram leases, by Mr. Dumergue who allowed a concession of 20 years' freedom from assessment on trees planted by the cowledars themselves and imposed a rental of only 10 palams per tree compared with 15 palams, the rent under other cowles.

G.O. No. 150, Pol., 29th Feb. 1892.

Cowles are still issued in the form sanctioned in 1885, but the terms under which the plots are actually held have since been modified in practice. The changes cannot be traced in the printed reports and it does not seem that they have ever been formally sanctioned. The paimashes have come to be made once in every twelve years. No use is now made of the first clause in the cowle to secure the assessment of young trees as they come into bearing. Instead, the assessment is imposed upon trees in bearing at the date of the paimash and is considered fixed and unalterable until the next paimash comes round. No reduction of assessment is granted except for the loss of trees by storm, lightning or other calamity. The present arrangement has the advantage over

Alterations in the original terms.

the old one of simplicity and is accepted by the people as a fair one.

The land was eagerly taken up during the years 1878—1884 and on Androth and Kalpeni planting proceeded rapidly so that now there is no jungle and almost no land left waste. But on the other islands the indolence of the cowledars who are mainly owners of a large number of private trees has prevented them from taking advantage of the benefits offered by the cowles. The period during which no assessment was to be charged has long since expired, yet in most cases little fresh planting has been done, and the number of trees is actually less than it was when the cowles were first granted. Kavarathi is the worst island in this respect. In 1847 there were 18,000 trees in the Pādhi Pādhi lands: in 1878 only 6,700, but in 1889 the number had fallen to 1,800. The consequent loss to the revenue is considerable. It was decided in 1908 and 1909 to attempt to improve matters in the interests both of Government and of the people by a system of mild coercion. The cowle lands on Kavarathi and Agathi were inspected, the number of trees that should be planted on the unplanted portions was calculated and lists showing how many trees each cowledar had to plant during the following year were given to the Amin with the warning that those who failed to plant the required number would be fined at the rate of Re. 1 for every 50 theis not planted. In a few instances only was the measure productive of some good. The greater portion of the land remains unplanted as before. As a result of the inspection of 1920 it was suggested that in those cases where half the number of trees has not been planted, the cowles should be cancelled and the available land given to deserving islanders of the poorer class who would be more likely to make a good use of it. This proposal was approved by Government and was carried out during the inspection of 1922, some 28 plots being granted on fresh cowles on Kavarathi.

Failure of the scheme.

Necessitates coercion.

The annual income derived from cowles is now about Rs. 5,500.

The uninhabited islands are Bitra, in the Amindivi Group, the two islets Valiyakara and Cheriyakara in the Suheli reef, Kalpitti, a small islet south of Agathi and within the same lagoon, and Bangaram Tinnakara and Parli, three islets in a lagoon about five miles north of Agathi, and Pitti, a mere sandbank belonging to the Malabar islands.

The uninhabited islands.

The Suheli islets belonged originally to the people of Kavarathi to whom the fisheries and cowry banks on the shoal were a valuable possession. They were confiscated by the Raja in 1765 in punishment of a suspected conspiracy and the murder of Hussein Kariyakar, the Raja's agent. Similarly the valuable fisheries of the Bangaram reef belonged to the people of Agathi but were confiscated in 1764 in punishment for the murder of an accountant who rendered himself obnoxious to the people by introducing the new monopolies. The other islands appear to have been recognised as Pandaram property from the earliest times.

These islands were strictly preserved by the Raja's Agents, no one being allowed ever to fish in the lagoons without permission or unaccompanied by a nadpal (peon). The nuts were collected intermittently by the Kariyakars on behalf of the Raja. The system was continued on the Malabar islands during the first few years of the attachment. Mr. Logan proposed in 1878 to introduce the cowle system upon the uninhabited islands also but this was not done. In 1880 Mr. Brodie proposed that the well planted islands, Bangaram Tinnakara and Parli should be eventually cleared of the dense jungle with which they were, and still are, covered, and leased out in blocks to the Agathi islanders. Meanwhile, as this scheme would take time, he leased the islands provisionally for three years to three Agathi men. At the same time, he also leased the Suheli islets pending the establishment of a colony from Kavarathi upon them. A previous attempt, made by Sir W. Robinson to settle upon Suheli some of the people left destitute after the great storm of 1846, failed owing to the impossibility of finding good water upon the islets, and for the same reason the people who offered to colonise them in 1880 also withdrew and refused to live on the islands but were prepared to take up land there. The system of leasing the islands was thus for one reason or another continued. Mr. Dumergue leased the Bangaram group in 1891 for 20 years, to the Agathi Amin for Rs. 1,000 with a condition that 500 theis should be planted annually. He also rented out Kalpitti for 20 years and allowed the previous lease of Suheli to continue. In 1892 the lease of Suheli was put up to public auction. In 1904 the Agathi Amin surrendered his lease of Bangaram and it was put up for public auction for five years, with a condition securing the planting of a certain number of theis each year. These terms have now been extended to all the islands. The leases are auctioned for five years and the purchaser binds himself to plant a stipulated number of theis during the period of his lease.

At the last auction for the lease 1920—25, Bangara Tinnakara and Parli fetched Rs. 2,745 per annum while Suheli for the same period realized Rs. 1,505. Pitti is only a sandbank.

It has been leased out since 1912 to the Gumastham of Kavarathi on an annual rent of Re. 1 but so far he has not succeeded in getting any coconut plants to grow upon the island. They have either been eaten away by crabs or pulled up by islanders visiting the spot.

Bitra.

A proposal was made to lease Bitra in 1870 but was objected to by the people who feared interference with their rights of fishing and of using certain communal trees. The island was, however, subsequently leased but only fetches about Rs. 11 per annum. An attempt was made between 1908 and 1912 to settle two families from Chetlat upon the island. Fifty trees were assigned to each, but the experiment failed.

South Kanara Islanders claim fishing rights.

The South Kanara islanders in 1895 claimed the right of fishing off the uninhabited Malabar islands and subsequently the Malabar islanders claimed the right of fishing at Bitra. The Collector of Malabar pointed out that there were difficulties in the way of allowing free fishing rights as the islands were leased out, while the right was mainly claimed for the object of plundering nuts, but at the same time he promised that South Kanara islanders should be given the same facilities as the Malabar islanders. In order to protect the renters, fishing passes were introduced. These were granted by the Amins of Agathi and Kavarathi who searched the boats on their return. This system, however, proved ineffectual to stop plundering and the renters suffered. The matter was enquired into in 1904. It was demonstrated that the sole object of the Ameni islanders in visiting the Malabar islands was to steal nuts, as the different shoals of their own group provided far superior fishing. It was decided in consequence to prohibit them altogether from fishing at either Suheli or Bangaram. Fishing passes continue to be granted by the Amins to their own islanders over whom there is naturally greater control.

G.O. No. 348, Pol., 8th June 1905.

Lesser monopolies.

It has been already stated that the Rajas placed a monopoly upon all the produce of the islands. Upon the very strong recommendations made by Sir W. Robinson, coconuts, morinda citron, limes, holothuria, salt and tobacco were released from the monopoly in 1859, but the monopolies upon tortoise-shell, ambergris, and cowries remained, and were continued by Government until recent years upon the Malabar islands. On the South Kanara islands the only monopoly was upon ambergris. It was found that the tortoise-shell and ambergris monopolies realized nothing at all in most years and only encouraged a system of smuggling, especially in the case of tortoise-shell which was not a monopoly upon the South Kanara islands. Recommendations to abolish them were made for many years and this was finally done in 1909

G.O. No. 96 Pol., 20th Feb. 1909.

so far as the Malabar islands were concerned. The ambergris monopoly upon the South Kanara islands followed in 1910.

G.O. No. 2855 Rev., 30th Aug. 1910.

The cowry monopoly was also abolished in 1910. Under the Rajas, it had been a source of considerable profit. Two seers of rice were, until 1826, paid for every seer of cowries; after that the price was reduced to one seer, and the consequent profits must have been nearly 400 per cent. The supply was not left to chance and if a sufficient quantity was not brought in voluntarily the people were forced to go out and gather. In this way the annual supply was maintained at from 10 to 12 candies. After the attachment of the islands, the price was fixed at 4 annas per seer. From that time the monopoly declined. Except on Kalpeni the supply seems to have decreased and it became impossible to gather the shells without an amount of labour out of proportion to the price paid. At the same time the market price and the demand steadily declined until eventually it was almost impossible to find a sale for even the small quantities brought in. In these circumstances this monopoly also was abolished.

Robinson I, p. 40. Robinson II, p. 40.

MINICOY.

The fiscal system on Minicoy is rather different. Except the land occupied by the village and a very small extent near it, the whole island was regarded as the Raja's jenmam property. In consequence no monopolies upon any of the produce of the island were ever imposed. The Pandaram Pāk was strictly preserved, the islanders were forbidden practically the whole island except the small portion near the village, which was leased out on Valiya pattom, and were cooped up within the village itself. They paid a poll tax (allara) of 20 lb. coir per man per head and of 5 lb. coir per head per woman, but the higher and richest class the Malikhans, one married woman in each family, all unmarried persons and toddy drawers were exempt. The tax was assessed by the Mukris. The allara is still levied and realizes between Rs. 500 and Rs. 800 per annum. It is now paid in cash at the rate of 12 annas on a married couple, 6 annas on an unmarried man and 4 annas on an unmarried woman.

The allara.

Taxes which only yielded petty sums were imposed upon the mas boats and upon vessels trading with Bengal. These were abolished in 1892.

Attiri pattom.

The lands held under Valiya pattom yield about Rs. 750. They are all held by a few Malikhans. The poorer people were allowed to cultivate the Attiri (sea-shore) Pandaram, a small strip on the western shore, north of the village, and paid a rent of 4 annas per tree (Attiri pattom). The Attiri land was not divided among them or demarcated in any way. As on the other islands, property consisted only of the trees and a man might plant a tree where he pleased on vacant ground in the Attiri Pandaram, subject only to payment of the assessment when the tree came into bearing. The villagers also possessed a little freehold land close to the village, the trees upon which paid no tax. The greater portion of the Raja's income was derived from the produce of the coconuts on the remainder of the island. The number of nuts collected varied with the season from a few thousand to one or two lakhs. The nuts in the Raja's time were only collected monthly after they had fallen to the ground. The fibre derived from nuts thus left to ripen and drop is coarser and poorer than if the nuts are plucked at the proper time, and the practice for many years now has been to pluck them. The people were remunerated in coconuts at a mamul rate for their labour in picking. The old mamuls with slight differences were paid until the new lease introduced by Mr. Innes and were as follows:— The Big South Pandaram.

Of every 124 nuts plucked, 20 were given to the Melacheri who plucked and 4 to the woman at the foot of the tree who gathered. Four nuts in addition were given to every man and woman for attending the plucking and six nuts if they also helped to carry the nuts to the cutcherry. Two Malikhans and two Malmis who were bound to attend to see that accounts were properly kept and that there was no stealing received 50 coconuts each. One or two Melacheri muppans or headmen might be present and would get 25 nuts each. If any nuts could not be carried to the cutcherry the same day, the men who were left to guard got 18 nuts each. When the nuts were taken by boat to the cutcherry each boatman got 14 to 18 nuts according to the distance. The Amin and gumasthan got 100 nuts each month in which plucking took place while the peons got 25 each. The persons who husked the nuts got 8 nuts per day and 4 nuts for every 100 husked. The steersmen who counted the nuts as they were loaded on to the "Odi" received 12 nuts each while the Odi Malmi (Captain) and another Malmi who supervised them received 50 nuts each. Rs. 2 to 2½ per thousand nuts was paid to the Odi owners as freightage. Out of the proceeds of the collections certain mamul religious charges amounting to 4,875 nuts had to be met. Mamuls for plucking.

Mr. Logan proposed to introduce his "improving leases" on Minicoy also. Owing, however, to the time occupied in surveying and leasing the other islands the work on Minicoy could not be taken until Mr. Underwood's visit in 1882. He divided the islands into nine blocks, and he granted cowles for the Attiri Pandaram and the lands held on Valiya pattom. Proposed introduction of cowles.

Causes friction.

It was the subsequent attempt of Mr. Dance in 1887 to complete the work and to give out cowles for the big Pandaram which led to the serious disturbance already narrated. The proposal to extend the cowle system any further was in consequence wisely dropped and the old arrangements were allowed to continue. But the system was not satisfactory. The share of the pluckings which Government received depended directly upon the honesty of the Amin and people. There could be no check upon them and if they combined to plunder Government it was almost impossible to detect them. The results were in many years most suspicious. In 1908 instead of a possible 1½ to 2½ lakhs only 4,800 were picked, an amount quite insufficient to meet even the mamuls detailed above so that Government's share for the year was a minus quantity. Rats undoubtedly do enormous damage but it is hard to believe that they alone were responsible and it was thought necessary to warn the islanders that if similar results occurred again, the cowle system would certainly have to be introduced. The result of this threat was that in 1909 over 2 lakhs of nuts were collected. The people it was noted were as strongly averse as ever to any system of cowles and the reasons seemed obvious. Even assuming—and it is to be feared that the assumption is a large one—that all nuts were honestly brought to account, the people had valuable communal rights in the Pandaram which would be destroyed by any system of cowles. They were allowed to cut trees past bearing for timber, free, and this is a valuable concession where coconut is the only wood in common use. They could also cut the firewood and collect the husks used in curing the mas, and they could cut the palm leaves which they use for thatching and fencing. Mr. Innes' liberal settlement after the disturbances of 1912 has put an end to this unsatisfactory state of affairs. As already stated above the South Pandaram is now leased to the islanders for 30 years at an annual rental of Rs. 1,552.

Poor results in some years of the pluckings.

In order to maintain the plantations, it was the rule for many years that the Amin should plant 3,000 "theis" in the Pandaram each year, but as the planting was done in any open space that presented itself, it was impossible to check his operations, while the dense jungle of screwpine remained undiminished in area. After 1908, it was proposed to do the planting systematically in blocks, the screwpine being first cleared so that the correct amount of planting could be insisted upon, while eventually it was hoped the whole Pandaram would be replanted and cleared of screwpine. Little progress had been made under the scheme up to 1912, but since the

New plantings.

Pandaram has come under the people's own management, energetic planting and clearing has been undertaken and it may reasonably be hoped that in a few years the Pandaram will become a very valuable property indeed.

Toddy tapping.

A small fluctuating income was derived from the rent paid by toddy tappers for Pandaram trees tapped by them. The toddy is used solely for the manufacture of sugar. Tappers paid a rent of two adubas of jaggery per tree. In the Raja's time all tappers whether they tapped private or Pandaram trees paid a poll tax of 24 adubas. In 1904, an attempt was made to encourage the jaggery industry. In that year in response to a request from the Raveries themselves, Mr. Cotton arranged for the tapping of 3,000 trees in the South Pandaram at a rate of 24 adubas per man per month. It was hoped that an income of at least Rs. 3,000 per annum would be realized. These tappers were established in two places in the South Pandaram but for some reason the scheme never succeeded and the tappers almost immediately began to agitate to be allowed to return to the village. In 1906 with the hope of accomplishing their object, they destroyed some young rubber trees planted at the lighthouse and were much chagrined at being ordered to remain in the Pandaram. In 1908, the threat to introduce cowles in consequence of the poor yield of nuts from the Pandaram gave them an excuse to abandon their settlements and they returned to the village, affecting to consider their tapping operations as the cause of the decrease in nuts. The scheme had never produced any large revenue and was no longer persisted in.

CHAPTER IV.

THE PEOPLE.

Their Manners, Customs and Laws.

The islanders, except on Minicoy, are all Moplahs almost indistinguishable in appearance and dress from the Moplahs of the mainland except that their physical development is very much better. On each island there are a few mainland Moplahs, usually young lads of the poorest classes, who have been brought over by the richer islanders on a mere living wage in order that their masters may evade payment of labour at higher customary rates prevailing on the islands. There are also usually one or two Hindus of the goldsmith castes from Malabar. The islanders themselves do not work in the precious metals and these mainland goldsmiths in consequence find a most remunerative business on the islands, returning after two or three years to the mainland with their earnings.

The population of each island, according to the latest figures (1921) is given in appendix II.

Religion.

The religion is Muhammadan. Like the Moplahs on the mainland, the islanders belong to the Shafi school of the Sunni sect and acknowledge, besides the Koran, the authority of the Sunneh or customary law as interpreted by Shafi. They are very strict in all their religious observances and have earned a great reputation for orthodoxy and piety among Muhammadans on the mainland. The men of Androth, particularly, pride themselves upon their religious knowledge and many of the Koyas of this island travel through Malabar giving religious instruction to the Moplahs and settling religious disputes.

On every island except Minicoy there are three public mosques to which all the islanders resort on particular occasions. These are the Jamath, Moidin and Ujira mosques. There are besides many small private mosques, out of all proportion in numbers to the inhabitants, each with its little tank and grave yard. On Minicoy there is no Ujira mosque. Some of the richer families on Ameni have small private mosques for the women to which the women of the neighbouring houses also come. In these mosques the imam is always a woman.

The Ramzan is strictly observed. Moiluths are performed in the month of Rabbil avvul (February-March) and three bethams or fasts are observed on the 13th, 14th and 15th of each lunar month.

On all the islands except Minicoy a curious religious exercise, the Zikkar, is performed in honour of the saint Seyid Ahamed every Sunday and Friday night, according to Muhammadan computation (i.e., every Saturday and Thursday night) in the Moidin and Ujira mosques. Regular bands of disciples, forty to sixty strong, are enrolled for these exercises and systematically trained, one of the recognised instructors being the head of the Sheikhindeveetil family at Androth. For the performance, the band seats itself in the mosque in two rows facing each other, each man with a kind of tambourine in his right hand. These two ranks perform a series of bending exercises, keeping in perfect time and beating time on their tambourines, while the half dozen principal performers dance up and down between the rows and work themselves into fits of real or pretended frenzy. At the end of each fit they leap into the air shouting "Seyid Ahamed Khabir, Seyid Ahamed Khabir," and strike their chests with all their might with large iron pins which have weighted wooden knobs rather like enormous skipping rope handles, or pass through both cheeks, or through lip and tongue, long iron skewers. The instruments used are terribly dirty and rusty but no ill effects seem to follow and little or no blood issues from the wounds. Another performer passes a blazing torch all over his body without apparently burning himself. Yet another, supported rigidly, by head and heels only, between two of the band, allows a fourth to strike lusty blows with a blunt sword upon his stomach without bending. These performances last for several hours.

Similar performances are given by the islanders on the mainland when they visit the coast and also by the Moplahs of Malabar, but on the mainland they are never allowed to take place in a mosque.

Language

The language of the people on the Laccadives proper is Malayalam with many peculiarities of pronunciation, idiom and vocabulary, which seem to be more pronounced in the more northern islands. The dialects spoken on Chetlat and Kiltan are particularly difficult to understand. The Malayalam P is universally pronounced as an F, and in the Amindivis the Malayalam "V" becomes "B" as in Kanarese. In the northern islands the interrogatory vowel appears to be ā instead of ō, while there are remains of a conjugation in personal endings similar to those used in the Tamil conjugations, which are sometimes employed. The Tamil words shollu, to say, and tanni, water, are in common use. A number of words apparently peculiar to the islands are in common use:

lacho and lachinni	sit down
imba	this side
amba	that side
chāla	much
subbeyku	in the morning
bimbi	ragi
chulāla	tender coconut
kōliyam	spider
koyēla	wages for climbing a tree
katti	jaggery
kattila	door frame
kīkare	seashore
pār	the reef
pāra	the sandstone found on most islands
pārum	coir soaking-pits on the seashore
arakan	a cock
alagam	a crab
bīr	contributions of rice by relatives and friends for a feast
balaga	matted fibre covering of a coconut stem
billam	lagoon
choppu	tobacco (evidently from the Kanarese "hogge sappu")
mādu	head
mādi	mid rib of coconut leaf.
miruga (corruption of mriga)	turtle
mattal	a rotten coconut
tōdi	coconut husk
thiggal	jungle.

They have also peculiar terms for the points of the compass: north Uttarandhi, north-east Shettandhi, east Purpandhi, south-east Thunarandhi, south Tekkandhi, south-west Birandhi, west Anarandhi, north-west Khajjandhi.

Minicoy. The inhabitants of Minicoy are Mahls, an entirely different race and speak a different language, Mahl, which is said to be allied to primitive Singalese. The inhabitants of the Maldives are also Mahls. In appearance they are strikingly different from the Malayalis of the Laccadives. The face is round and flat and is considered to be a primitive

Singalese type modified to some extent by an admixture of Arab blood.

On Ameni the people are divided into four classes:—(1) Tarawad, (2) Tanakampranavar, (3) Kudiyatis and (4) Melacheries. About 5 per cent of the population belong to the first, 35 per cent to 40 per cent to the second, 5 per cent to the third, and the remainder to the last class. The distinction between them appears to have been based originally upon property. The Tarawad class consisted of the four original tarawad families, Pondambelli, Porakat, Beyamada and Thupekal (now represented by the Poradan family), which alone in the early days of the settlement had tenants. The Tanakampranavar, as their name indicates, were those possessing independent property of their own but with no tenants under them. The Kudiyatis were originally the tenant class. The Melacheries were the landless tree climbers. Now, however, the Kudiyatis and even some Melacheries have acquired property of their own and all except the Melacheries have tenants. The first two classes can intermarry and intermarriage between them and the Kudiyatis is allowed, but has very seldom taken place. The women, however, of the Porakat family and its branches in remembrance of an old insult offered to a Porakat lady by a Tanakampranavan do not marry Tanakampranavars, although a Porakat man will marry a Tanakampranavan girl. Intermarriage for both classes with the Melacheries is strictly prohibited. In one case, a Tanakampranavan who married a Melacheri girl was outcasted. Intermarriage between the third and the fourth class is allowed. Classes Ameni.

Members of the Tarawad families emigrated to the Malabar islands and founded families there. Thus the extinct Idiyyakal family at Kavarathi was a branch of the Pondambelli family, while the Ārenākāda and Pudiyedan families are branches of the extinct Ameni family of Pudiyan. So also the Pātakal family at Androth is a branch of the Pondambelli, and the Manmel Tarawad of Kalpeni is a branch of the Tupekal family. The Ameni Tarawad families will intermarry with these related families and also with the Karanavar class on the Malabar islands but not with the other classes.

On Chetlat, Kiltan and Kadamath, with the exception of one family at Kiltan, the people are all Melacheries who have migrated either from Ameni or from the coast. On these northern islands those Melacheries who can read the Koran are styled Mukris and do not climb trees. One family at Kiltan which emigrated from Agathi many generations ago is not regarded as Melacheri and always holds the Khaziship of the island. On both Chetlat and Kiltan a few of the leading families style themselves Koyas and dress in rather better fashion but intermarry with the other Melacheri families. Their superior standing is not recognized by the Ameni islanders and when they visit that island, they have to conform to the custom regarding Melacheri dress.

Malabar islands.

On the Malabar group the people are divided into three classes, the Koyas, Malmis, and Melacheries. In the older reports the Malmis are also called Urukars but this term is now quite unknown and never used. The Koya families use the title of Koya, own most of the trees upon the islands and most of the odams. Some of the Malmis also are jenmies but usually on a smaller scale than the Koyas. Most of them are tenants. The Melacheries are petty tenants and servants of the other two classes and also toddy drawers. Intermarriage between the different classes is almost unknown. The Koyas of Androth, Kavarathi and Kalpeni claim to be descended from Nambudri and Nair ancestors from the coast and hence these three islands are known as Tarawad islands in distinction to Agathi, a Melacheri island, the inhabitants of which seem to have descended from Tiyyars and other lower castes. The three classes now existing on Agathi seem to have arisen in imitation of the distinctions which existed on the Tarawad islands. On Kavarathi and Androth are branches of a family, the Sheikhindeveetil family, which claims descent from the original Sheikh or descendant of the Prophet who came to Androth some six generations ago. The members rather regard themselves as a people apart from the rest of the islanders.

The Koyas or Tarawadis are the leisured class and rarely do any work. Occasionally they may do a little cultivation and fishing. Those who own odams superintend the repair of their vessels and sail their vessels to the coast and back. On the coast it is they who do all the trading with the dallals in the cargo shipped in their boats. The custom is to hand over the whole cargo to the particular dallal with whom the odam owner is in the habit of dealing, the dallal for his part maintaining the owner and his crew during their stay. Bitter complaints are made by the odam owners that the dallals keep large fictitious debts pending against them in their accounts and make adjustments and debits which the owners have no means of checking. The kudians, on the other hand, who are bound by island custom to ship their goods in their jenmi's odam or in the odam in which the jenmi himself ships, are equally loud in their complaints against the odam owners. The owners never used to render any account whatever and were proved to have had a secret compact with the dallals by which the notified price of all articles purchased was always less than the price paid to the owners. In order to protect the kudians to some extent an order was passed in 1909 that the odam owners when obtaining their port clearance should file in the Amin's office a copy of the list ordered in 1908 to be maintained showing the names of shippers and the quantities of goods shipped by each.

The Koyas make over most of their trees to tenants, either Malmis or Melacheries, who in return are bound to render certain customary services and pay a nominal rent.

In addition to the rules regarding intermarriage, certain distinctions in sumptuary matters are very strictly enforced on all the islands by the two higher classes. A Melacheri is not allowed to wear sandals or a jacket or coat or to use an umbrella. Only Melacheries can be barbers, goldsmiths or blacksmiths and only Melacheries may climb trees, carry loads, twist coir, or bale water and cook on the odams during a voyage. There seems to be a growing tendency on the part of the higher classes to enforce these distinctions more strictly while the Melacheries are demanding greater freedom. The class feeling has been very acute, particularly on Agathi and Androth. On Androth the Melacheries are an industrious and prospering class and naturally chafe at the subordination in which they are held by the Koyas. On Agathi strife between the two classes has been going on for some years past, mainly over the question whether Melacheries should be invited to sing in the singing parties at Koya weddings. This dispute first arose some 30 or 40 years ago. It was settled then by the formation of two singing parties of trained men both Koyas and Melacheries which were to be invited to all weddings. Gradually, however, on the score of expense some Koyas failed to invite the Melacheri members. Disputes arose in consequence. Mr. Rabjohns in 1913 gave a ruling upholding the old custom but the matter was taken in appeal to the High Court and failing to get a reconsideration of the order there, the aggrieved parties produced a situation upon the island which bordered upon anarchy. Melacheries refused to do any work for Koyas and even among the Koyas themselves dissensions arose. The dispute was happily compromised in 1920.

The people wear the same dress as Moplahs on the mainland. The cutcherry Karanavars, particularly on Androth, wear when in court and on ceremonial occasions long handsome robes of silk or velvet of any brilliant hue that takes their fancy, with a finely embroidered waistcoat underneath. Dress.

The women do not observe gosha. Their ornaments are much like those of Moplah women in Malabar. They are of gold in the case of the higher castes and of silver for the Melacheries. The ears are pierced at regular intervals just inside their outer rim and from 12 to 15 earrings are usually worn. The earrings consist of a circle of fine gold or silver wire with a thin crescent of the same metal soldered inside it at one side and often beautifully worked. The richer women also wear high collarets of gold on ceremonial occasions. The men wear small oblong silver amulets containing a text from the Koran, tied either to the upper arm or to the waist string, as a charm.

Marriage. Boys are generally married between the ages of 18 and 20, girls when they are between 10 and 12, but a fatherless girl cannot be married until she has attained puberty. The first match is arranged for a boy by the karanavars of both parties. Subsequent marriages he is allowed to arrange for himself. The ceremony performed is the usual Muhammadan nikka ceremony. It is usually performed in the bride's house if she belongs to the upper classes and in the mosque if she is a Melacheri. The customary dowry by the husband to the wife is Rs. 30 for the first class, Rs. 12 for the second and from Rs. 3 to 6 for Melacheries. Rich families spend very large sums on the feast which accompanies a wedding. Very rich families will even feast the whole island, and 15 to 20 muras of rice, 8 or 10 cows, some 20 goats and 5 or 6 maunds of jaggery will be consumed. The whole expenditure falls in the first instance upon the bride's family. After the public feasting, the relatives and friends who accompany the bridegroom are feasted for seven days at the bride's house. Among the upper classes the bridegroom is conducted to the bride's house with singing. The Melacheries are allowed to have singing only in their houses and not on the way. The songs (kettipadu) sung on these occasions are either composed locally for the occasion or are printed Moplah songs brought over from the mainland. The bride's house is of course greatly decorated for the occasion. The bridegroom brings with him two companions (tholi) who stay with him at the bride's house for the next forty days. After the marriage the bridegroom has to make a customary present to the bride of a fixed number of cloths and saries, which in the case of the higher classes is quite a costly gift. It is, however, collected by the bridegroom from among his relations, he having to give back to each when his turn comes to get married a cloth of equal value.

Although the initial expenditure for the wedding falls upon the bride's family, the bridegroom has to reimburse them according to a customary scale a year later. This he does under a remarkable system of co-operative borrowing. He collects rice from all his relatives and friends on condition of repayment to them free of interest later under similar circumstances. Such a contribution of rice on condition of repayment upon the occasion of some ceremony in the lender's house is known as a bīr. It is a recognised system of borrowing. Regular accounts of the transactions are kept. If the loans are not repaid, the amounts are recoverable by suit and they can form the subject of a vasiyath to children or anandiravans.

Bīr.

A man always sleeps in his wife's house (vidu), takes tea or kunjee there in the early morning and then goes to his own house (pura). All his meals he takes in his own house.

Divorce.

Divorce is very common and in most cases it appears to be the woman who wants it. If the wife does not want the husband, he is bound to divorce her, but may take back all the clothing and jewelry which he has given her and also a portion of the bīr. If the husband wants the divorce, he, has to relinquish to the wife all that he may have given her, including the mahar. Either party can divorce for any reason whatever. As might be expected, with these facilities for divorce on both sides, very few men have more than one wife and there are very few men or women who have not been married and divorced several times.

Birth ceremonies.

On the birth of the first child, the father gives the wife's family 11 muras of rice for expenses, 15 bottles of coconut oil and 40 fowls, all collected on the bīr system. The mother observes no particular ceremonies. On the seventh day the father or grandfather gives the child its name but there is no ceremony. On the fortieth day the child's head is first shaved and the father usually gives a small feast in honour of the occasion. Circumcision takes place when a boy is between 7 and 10 years old, but if the father is poor and unable to find the money for the customary feast which is given on the occasion, it may even be postponed till the boy is 15. The rite is performed by a specially skilled barber. There is no religious ceremony. The father gives a feast to relatives and friends or if he is a rich man, entertains the whole island. For girls an ear-boring ceremony has been performed in a few cases within recent years, but it is quite an innovation. It takes place when the girls are between the ages of 5 and 10. The boring is performed by one of the women or by a goldsmith.

Death ceremonies.

After death, the body is first washed and then anointed with scents. The eyes are closed and antimony applied round them. A preparation of camphor and benzol is applied to the eyes, nose, ears and mouth. The body is then wrapped in three pieces of cloth, laid in the coffin and tied in with three strips of cloth, one at the head, one at the waist and one at the feet. Each relative provides four cubits of cloth for these purposes. Only a small portion of the cloth contributed is, however, actually used for wrapping the body. Rich people dress the body in turban, jacket, and cloth. The coffin is finally placed on a cot under a canopy. The burial takes place as soon as possible, but before the body is carried to the grave, a feast is given, in the case of rich people to the whole island. A peculiarity of the feasting is the free distribution of uncooked rice also, particularly to the richer people present. All the rice for these presents and for the feast is collected under the bīr system. After the burial, mukrics read the Koran at the grave or in the house for 3, 7 or 11 days and on the last day of the reading there is another feast.

Beautifully carved tomb stones of coral lime a stone stained a delicate green or blue and bearing texts from the Koran are set up at head and foot of the grave. The tomb stones carved on Kavarathi are particularly fine.

As might be expected among sea-faring folk the building of an odam is attended with feasting and ceremonial. A feast is given to the carpenters when the keel is laid. At the launching, moulath is read, prayers are said and there is much singing by both men and women separately. A large feast is given and the persons attending it bring gifts to the owner for which he is expected to give an equivalent when they in their turn build an odam.

Feasting Clubs.

Very ancient institutions, found also among the Moplahs of Malabar, are the feasting clubs. Each has a membership of 20 or 30 and each member contributes a small sum of money, a seer of rice and some coconuts. The keenest rivalry exists between the various clubs, each trying to outdo the other in the sumptuousness of its repasts. One club will invite the members of another club to a feast and that club will in its turn invite the members of the first club to a feast which it will endeavour to make more spendid and more lavish than the feast given to it.

Law.

The island law is a curious mixture of the ordinary Muhammadan Law with the Marumakkattayam Law of Malabar. Property is regarded as either ancestral or self acquired

Ancestral property is known as Velliaricha (literally Friday property), pronounced Belliaricha on the Amindivis. Self acquired property is known as Tingalaricha (literally Monday property) on the Malabar islands and as Bēlaricha on the South Kanara islands. The reason for applying these terms to the different kinds of property is quite unknown. Velliaricha property is governed by the ordinary Marumakkattayam Law, i.e., descent is through a sister's children, while Tingalaricha property passes to a man's own children under the ordinary Muhammadan Law. The distinction as may be imagined leads to innumerable disputes which are often very difficult of decision. On the Amindivis, if a man has no sons he can constitute his Bēlaricha property the Belliaricha property of his daughters who become a tarwad within the tarwad so far as hereditary rights to that particular property are concerned. On the Amindivis ancestral property can be the subject of a mortgage but the right of redemption is reserved to the reversioners at the rate of Re. 1 per tree.

There was until recent years no idea of property in land. The property consisted entirely of the trees or houses upon the land. A man had a right to plant a coconut in any vacant space provided he did not do so within a recognized distance of an existing tree within which the owner of the tree had exclusive right to plant. It is difficult to say how far even now an idea of property in land has developed. All trees bear their owner's property mark and it is still a particular number of trees, not particular land, that is given to a tenant. On the other hand, there is a growing tendency to demarcate the ground and to define plots of trees by boundaries in documents.

The old system of planting has resulted in an extraordinary mixing up of properties, one man's trees being mixed up with another's in a way that is a fertile cause of disputes and adds considerably to the difficulty of setting them.

The customs, regarding tenancies are peculiar and almost feudal in character. The owners make over most of their trees to tenants (kudians), who pay a rent of one-tenth of the produce and are bound to render service to the jenmi. From 30 to 50 trees usually constitute a service but one man may hold several such grants from the same jenmi or from several jenmis. The more important services to be rendered by the kudian are to sail one trip in the jenmi's odam if he has one, or if not, in that odam in which the jenmi's ships his produce, to sail in the jenmi fishing boat, to thatch the odam shed, to paint and oil with fish oil the jenmi's odam and fishing boats, to serve in the jenmi's house at festivals and to thatch it.

In addition the kudian is bound to ship his goods in the jenmi's odam or in that odam in which the jenmi himself ships his goods, and he has to pay a freightage of one-tenth the value of goods shipped. The Koyas are extremely jealous of these rights, particularly those relating to the shipping of produce which give them a monopoly of the island trade. The kudians have always asserted their right to ship the produce of trees of which they are themselves the owners in any odam they please, and this right has been upheld by the Courts.

In default of service the owner can sue before the amin. Rs. 18 is the recognised amount at which one service is valued. On Ameni a distinction is drawn between Pale Kudians who have held trees under the same jenmis for many generations, and whose tenure is practically permanent, and Pudiya Kudians, holding more recent grants. Suits against Pale Kudians are usually only brought for enforcement of service, not for eviction.

Minicoy. The people of Minicoy are entirely different in manners and customs from the Malayali inhabitants of the Laccadives. Like them, they are all Muhammadans. They are divided

Classes. into four classes, the Rāvēris who are tree climbers and tappers and correspond to the Melacheries; the Takkrus, sailors and boatmen whose women use the title bibi; Mālmis, also sailors but of a better standing socially; and Mālikhāns, the highest class, corresponding to Koyas. The Mālmi women use the title bīfān and the Mālikhan women the title manikka. Intermarriage between Mālikhans and Mālmis and between Takkrus and Rāvēris is allowed but not between the two higher classes and the two lower. In former times the children of a marriage of a Takkru with a Rāvēri were known as Kōhlus, but this term has gone out of use within the last 30 or 40 years and the children of such a marriage now take the class of the father or mother whichever is higher. Interdining is only allowed between the classes between which intermarriage is allowed and in fact the caste system is complete. Intermarriages with the higher classes on the other islands and with Moplahs from the mainland occasionally take place.

Courtship is a recognised preliminary to marriage. Early marriages are not allowed. Men do not marry before they are 20 years of age and women not until they are 16. The people are strict monogamists in theory and in practice, and divorces are quite uncommon. In these respects they are markedly superior to the inhabitants of the Laccadives proper.

Inheritance. The laws of inheritance are peculiar. Owing to the monopoly of practically all the land by the Bibi, the houses form almost the only kind of real property known. Island law decrees that no man can have any claim to a house. It vests in the women of the family and the men of the family have only the right of residence and maintenance till marriage. On marriage a man passes to his wife's house and takes his wife's family name. A woman who ceases to reside in the family house for any reason *ipso facto* loses her claim to reside in it and cannot return. Other property follows the ordinary Muhammadan laws of succession.

Sanitary laws.

From time immemorial certain sanitary rules have been observed. All small-pox cases are segregated on the little island of Viringilli immediately south of the main island and all cases of leprosy, as soon as they are pronounced by the Khazi to be leprosy, are sent to a Leper Settlement about a mile north of the village where the unfortunate persons remain for the rest of their lives. Public opinion so strongly supports these customs that, although no guards are posted over either Settlement, no escapes are ever attempted.

Social customs.

In social matters the development of the Minicoy islanders is equally marked. The village is divided into nine wards or attiris. Each has its club for the men, and its corresponding varangi for the women. Each attiri or vārangi has its own club house. The men's club house is an unpretentious affair, sometimes an ugly corrugated iron structure, simply furnished with one or two large swinging divans on which the men can sit and swing themselves as they talk. Here the attiri feasts take place and all the necessary saman is ranged on shelves round the walls. Each attiri maintains at a very considerable expense a troupe of dancers, a snake boat, and a jolly boat Each troupe of dancers is from 40 to 50 strong and though the dress of all the troupes is similar, each attiri has its own distinctive colour. The dress consists of a pair of coloured silk trousers cut very wide at the feet, a white cloth with a red border tied round the waist and hanging down almost to the ankles and two coloured silk clothes tied round the waist so as to leave a triangular point hanging down behind. Scarlet waist strings with long beaded tassels and a mother of pearl pocket knife with silver ornaments are worn by the rank and file, while the leaders are distinguished by handsome velvet sabre-taches of blue or scarlet edged with silver lace. The upper part of the body is naked. On the head a small coloured cap is worn with a silk cloth tied tightly into a roll and wound round it to form a brim. In the waist, in the cap, and hanging from it down the back are sprays of the betel vine which add a most effective touch to the costume. The only music is provided by a small barrel-shaped drum which each man has slung from his neck and on which he keeps perfect time in even the most complicated exercises. A complete costume costs from one hundred to two hundred rupees and is provided by the wearer himself. All the dances are performed with marvellous precision. Some are of a most exhausting character and leave the performers at the end breathless and exhausted.

The snake boats or jeha dhonies are beautiful craft, built on exquisite lines. and very fast. They are long enough to accommodate eleven or twelve pairs of rowers and just wide enough for two men to sit abreast. They have a small platform at the stern on which the coxswain stands, while a man with a paddle sits at his feet on each side and gives the time to the rowers. The crews are dressed uniformly, each attiri having its own distinctive colour for turban and trousers, the boats and oars are gaily painted, and the appearence of the whole fleet is striking. Each attiri also maintains a large jolly boat painted to match its snake boat, which is used to tow important visitors ashore or out again to their ship or for trips in the lagoon. A snake boat race is usually held when an Inspecting Officer visits the island and creates much enthusiasm.

Each attiri is ruled by a headman appointed by the attiri but there seems to be no definite election or appointment. The post is not hereditary and a holder is deposed as soon as he loses the confidence of the attiri. Each headman has an assistant. All affairs relating to the attiri are settled in public meeting known as a Vēmādu which is summoned by the headman. Questions affecting the whole island are discussed and settled at a meeting of all the attiris known as a Havar.

The women of each ward are similarly organised under a headwoman. The club house, Vārangi, is beautifully built on the model of an old-fashioned sailing-ship's State room. The men provide all the money and labour required for the building. The walls are often neatly panelled in wood or are tastefully decorated with painted designs, and the whole building shows more real artistic taste and perfection of execution than is usually to be met with in buildings on the mainland. Round the walls runs a low masonry seat. Here the Vārangi meets to discuss its affairs and here during the day the women bring their coir and sit twisting it and gossiping while their babies play about upon the floor.

The women seem to enjoy almost as much freedom as European women. The men are mainly serangs and kalassis upon ships and are away from the island for 2 or 3 years at a time. As a result the women have acquired considerable influence in public affairs and it is usual to consult them in matters affecting the island. There is no school on the island and it is the women of each family who teach the children to read and write Mahl. There are separate bathing tanks for the women. Men are not allowed to approach them on the shady places behind the village where the women beat out the coir.

The ordinary dress of a Minicoy man consists of a turban of red cloth with a large chequered pattern of narrow white lines upon it, a pair of white or butcher's-blue trousers and a white cloth tied round the waist and falling to well below the knees. The upper part of the body is bare. When out fishing in their mas boats, the men wear cloth hats of all colours and of extraordinary shapes which give them a most picturesque appearance. Dress.

The women of the upper classes wear, over fine silk cloths similar to those worn by the richer Moplah women, a long red silk overall with short sleeves, opening only at the neck where it is fastened together by two loops, one on each shoulder. The silk is of a particular kind which is brought from Bengal. The hair is worn in a peak at the back of the head and over this is tied a dark blue kerchief covering the head. Only the three upper classes may wear gold or silver ornaments. The Manikkas wear a number of gold rings in the outer rim of the ear rather as the Moplah women do. The other two classes wear silver. On festive occasions the arms are covered with silver armlets from wrist to elbow.

The Rāvēri women wear a similar overall of the same colour but of coarser silk. They wear dark kerchiefs on their heads and tie the hair in a kind of big chignon at the back and slightly to one side. They are not allowed to wear earrings of gold or silver but have the rims of the ears pierced like the other classes and wear small rings of dark thread in them.

Every woman carries a fine betel pouch plaited in Ceylon or the Maldives from a particular grass. Inside are a small pair of arecanut cutters and a conical silver casket with two compartments, one containing chunam and the other arecanut or tobacco. From the casket hangs a long handsome silver chain at the end of which are attached sets of silver implements for cleaning the teeth and ears. The bridegroom on marriage is expected to give the bride a complete set, a plaited pouch and silver box with its pendant.

The houses on Minicoy are better built and more lofty than on the Laccadives proper but are very dark, windows being few and small. A long verandah runs down the outside from which the rooms open. A prominent feature in Houses.

each room is a large swinging couch of the kind already mentioned as being found in the men's attiris, and in each corner will be seen suspended the mosquito curtains of long-cloth, within which the inmates are forced to shelter themselves from the hordes of mosquitoes that infest the island.

A curious ceremony takes place when the Inspecting officer or Collector visits the island. The women of the island march to the cutcherry by vārangis to pay their respects. All range themselves round and then representatives of each vārangi advance. The first two women carry rose water sprinklers filled with rose water or other scented water with which the guests are liberally sprinkled. The next woman anoints the guests with attar or sandalwood oil. A fourth advances bearing an electroplate egg-stand and a tea pot. Into the egg cups she pours a sweetened drink from the tea pot, and presents them. A fifth presents the time-honoured pan supari, a sixth a bowl of eggs and a seventh a fowl or two. The same ritual is gone through by each of the nine vārangis in turn.

The coconut husk is beaten only on Saturday, Sunday, Tuesday, and Thursday in each week although twisting may be done on any day. If a death occurs in a Malikhan family, beating is stopped by the family for three days, if in a family belonging to one of the other classes, for one day. Similarly, if any person is declared a leper and sent to the settlement, beating is stopped for three days.

CHAPTER V.

OCCUPATIONS AND TRADE.

Boat-building.

The islanders are expert boat builders. The "lines" of their boats are quite different from any followed by builders on the coast or from those of Arab vessels which now ply to coast ports, and seem to have been evolved by the people themselves. Nothing at all approaching their boats in excellence of construction and in beauty is to be found upon the mainland. The wood is all brought from the mainland and wrought upon the islands. On the Laccadives proper the planks are sewn together with coir twine and caulked. The boats are tarred, and treated subsequently at intervals with fish oil. The big coast-going vessels (odams) are undecked but have a narrow planking amidships, under a roofing of coconut matting which affords some shelter to the crew, and a small platform at the stern for the helms man. The boat's sides at the stern are somewhat raised and they and the stern itself are elaborately decorated with arabesque patterns and scroll work in white chunam. They have one mast and carry one large latteen-shaped sail and a jib. The rowing boats have short curiously flimsy oars consisting of a small round paddle tied on to a coconut shaft. The oars are tied to tholepins with coir twine which is continually breaking. The islanders however are expert rowers and can row the long distances between island and island without more rest than is afforded by the continual breaking of the tholepin cords.

A few boats are built on Chetlat for sale to other islands. On most islands, however, only boats required for the island itself are constructed.

Minicoy.

In the science of boat building Minicoy is in advance even of the Laccadives. The timbers are all pegged together or nailed and not sewn. Instead of being merely tarred, the mas boats and jeha boats are artistically painted in colours. In earlier times small quaintly rigged brigs used to be built and the famous Dom Malikhan had a small fleet of them. Some of these vessels are still afloat but no new ones have been built of recent years.

Fishing.

As is only to be expected a considerable amount of fishing is done on all the islands but there is no export of fish on any large scale except from Minicoy. Outside the reef practically all the fishing is by hook and line, nets being hardly ever used. The line is made of white cotton cord, never tanned, which the islanders themselves twist from cotton brought from the mainland, and is furnished with two hooks. The baits mainly used are hermit crabs and siphunculids.

Inside the lagoon, nets are used. Three kinds are known, the kandalai vala, the adi vala and the vīsu vala. The kandalai vala is the largest net used. It is made in sections. Each section belongs to several men and the owners of all or a number of sections unite for fishing. This net is made of untanned cotton, spun on the island, with 1¼ inch meshes in the wings decreasing to 7/8th meshes at the centre. The float line is buoyed by cylindrical floats of "paruthi," a white wood, threaded on at close intervals. The first process in the operation of fishing with this net is to lay out an "ōla vala," a coir rope to which have been tied narrow strips of coconut leaf as thickly as possible all along its length. This is also made in sections by separate owners who unite for the fishing. The "ōla vala" is coiled into two boats which proceed side by side a considerable distance into the lagoon. When they get sufficiently far from shore the boats separate and return to the shore in a wide sweep, paying out the ōla vala as they go and also distributing their crews at intervals along it till there is only one man left to work the boat. The men thus jettisoned swim or wade behind the "ōla vala" to lift it over any rocks and once the ends have reached the shore keep up a continuous shouting to scare the fish and prevent them breaking through. When the boats get near enough, other men from the shore dash into the water, catch the ends of the rope, drag them ashore, and commence pulling the rope in. The bight of the rope is thus gradually narrowed. More men dash in and take station along it, till finally a small piece of water is completely enclosed by a ring of shouting men lined along the rope, and the "catch" can be seen dashing frantically through the water in attempts to escape. The kandalai vala is now taken out in a boat to the furthest point from the shore and paid out equally from there along both sides, inside the rope, till it completely encloses the space. It is then dragged ashore with much shouting. The catch is divided up among the owners of the sections, and those who have helped. The kandalai vala is the net used on the fishing expeditions to the great reefs.

The adi vala is a small seine net used only in very shallow water. It has wooden floats of "Paruthi" and along the bottom small coral stones as weights. It is 18 fathoms long by five or six feet deep.

The vīsa vala is a simple cast net, used generally only from the shore and not from a boat as on the coast. It has no strings, is of untanned cotton and is weighted with elongated leads strung along its margin. Sometimes these leads are neatly fashioned in the form of a half moon.

Fish are also caught by spearing or harpooning from a boat. There are two kinds of harpoons, used for different kinds of fish. In one, the "chattuli," used mainly by day or for big fish at night, the head is of iron, single barbed, with a socket in the base fitting over an iron pin at the end of the shaft, so that when a big fish is struck the iron head is detached. To the head is securely tied a length of coir rope and this is tied also to the shaft and then coiled in the boat. When a big fish is struck the head with the rope attached is left in, the shaft probably becoming detached and the fish is eventually pulled in by the rope when tired out. The other harpoon the "chillu" consists of a bundle of fine coconut prongs tied on the end of a light shaft. A coir cord is tied to the other end of the shaft and then round the harpooner's wrist. This is used when torch fishing by night, mainly for the gar fish, or by day for flying fish. It is much used at sunset on Kavarathi for gar fish inshore, the harpooners wading out into the water and standing motionless till a fish approaches. This kind of harpoon is also used for night fishing by torchlight in South Kanara.

For harpooning by day a false bait (poi-mīn) is used. It is a wooden dummy in the shape of a fish, 10 or 12 inches long, painted black, with white lines and markings of chunam and a white rag tied to its tail. A man standing in the bow plays the poi-mīn on the surface by means of a short rod and line in his left hand while in his right he holds the harpoon ready to strike as soon as a fish makes a rush for the bait. By night a torch is used and the fish, attracted to the light are speared, the appropriate harpoon being used.

On all the islands, but most largely on Kavarathi, ingenicus fish traps are used. These are of rough wicker and heart shaped, with an opening so contrived that a fish once in cannot get out. They are not baited at all but are placed on the lagoon bottom with stones built up round them so as to make it appear that they are simply holes in the rocks. The unsuspecting fish enters and is caught. They are of all sizes from quite small ones to cages five or six feet long by four feet high. Small rafts are used for placing them in position and examining them.

Mas-fishing on Minicoy

On Minicoy the bonito or Mas-fishing forms an important and valuable industry. Special boats are used. These are particularly large fast-sailing boats, with a broad platform over-hanging the stern. Just forward and just aft of the single mast are two wells in the bottom of the boat in which the live bait used is kept. Each well has a hole leading into it through the boat's side, through which a continuous stream of water spouts. The ends of the wells are formed of boards with perforations through which the water overflows from the wells into the bottom of the boat; and all the time the boat is at sea two men with copper bailers are continuously occupied in baling out the water which overflows. The boat carries two sails, a large square sail of matting, rigged to a cross yard which when lowered is rested on a crutch at the stern, and a sprit sail made of cotton fabric. The gun-wales are built up rather high at the bows where they are pierced for the oars. The crew consists of 15 to 20 men and a number of boys. Twelve of these boats belong to the attiries and for each, one muppan and three men are appointed for the year. Twenty per cent of the catch goes to the attiri fund, the rest is distributed among the crews. The remaining six boats belong to single individuals who maintain a standing crew of four, responsible to them for the management and manning of the boat: the rest of the crew are volunteers secured by these four for each trip.

The live bait used is of two kinds, a small minnow, and a larger fish about the size of a big sardine. It is caught in the lagoon and is kept till wanted in special baskets which are floated in the lagoon. The rods used are six feet bamboos with a line of the same length. The hook is a barbless iron hook, with the shank made broad and flat and curved to resemble a small fish. It is kept freshly coated with lead to make it bright. When the boat gets into a shoal every available hand seizes a rod and crowds on to the platform leaving only the malmi to steer and three or four boys to manage the big mat sail. One bailer stops bailing and catching the live bait in a kind of sieve throws some out on each side to attract the fish. A scene of indescribable excitement ensues. While the bailer hurls the live bait right and left among the fish, two men on each side keep up a continuous splashing with long wooden ladles. The others dash their hooks among the shoal and as soon as they get a bite, haul out the fish by main force, swing it on board, and with a deft dip of the rod, all in one motion, unhook it and send it slithering between their legs down the platform into the well of the boat. A shoal may remain from five to ten minutes round the boat and then departs as quickly as it came, but in the time 70 or 80 fish will have been captured.

When the boats return in the evening, the fish are cleaned. The gill covers are wrenched off by hand and then the mouth parts and viscera are easily pulled out. Then comes the division of the catch. The boat owner gets 21 out of every 100, while the standing crew get half as much again of the remainder as the volunteers. Each man takes his share home where the women at once proceed deftly to trim off what remains of the head and to fillet the fish. They cut it first vertically into two along the spine removing the spine and fins. Then each of these large pieces is cut down the middle into two fillets. The fillets are washed in two changes of water and then boiled for 12 hours in equal parts of fresh and salt water. Next morning they are taken out and laid in a single layer over smouldering coconut husks and allowed to smoke for a couple of hours. They are then spread on coconut mats in the sun and allowed to dry till so hard that they will not yield to the touch. This requires about three days. The dried fish is sold to traders on the island who ship it to Ceylon either direct or via Calicut or Cannanore. The price realised is three or four annas a fillet and in a good year the industry is estimated to bring in about Rs. 25,000.

Bêche-de-mer or Trepang.

This delicacy so greatly appreciated by the Chinese was at one time very largely manufactured on the islands. It is made from the holothurian or sea cucumber of which three suitable varieties are found, the vella kōkā, mottled grey and brown, the karutha kōkā, black, and the soganna kōkā reddish brown. The animals are found in great quantities in the lagoons of all the islands and are collected by wading and also by spearing from a boat.

The curing process is as follows:—Each holothurian is first cut open longitudinally and the viscera removed; the thick fleshy body wall remaining is washed in sea water and then boiled for not less than half an hour till a characteristic odour is given off. The pieces are then taken out of the pot pinned open with short wooden skewers to prevent curling and dried in strong sunlight upon a cadjan platform for 7 days. They are then packed and exported mainly to Ceylon through Mangalore middlemen. The price is about Rs. 5 per thulam of 28 lb. With improved methods of curing, the industry appears capable of considerable expansion.

Coir twisting.

The important industry of coir twisting is carried on only by the women of the Melacheri class. The coconuts are plucked and husked by the men. The husks are then left to steep for six or eight months in pits built with coral rock between high and low water-mark in sheltered situations on either the lagoon beach or the sea beach. A few fresh water pits in the interior of the island are also used but the coir from husks soaked in fresh water is not considered to be so good. When sufficiently rotted, the husks are taken out and beaten by the women with a wooden beater on a flat stone. The resulting coir is then washed out and dried and finally twisted by the women by hand into yarn. Feet as well as hands are cleverly used. The quality depends upon the fineness of the twist and the colour. The best Laccadive coir is produced on Chetlat but on Minicoy a very fine twist is produced which is very greatly superior to it.

Jaggery and vinegar. The people being Muhammadans are not allowed by their religion to drink fermented toddy but a considerable amount of tapping for sweet toddy is done. Instead of coating the pots with lime to prevent fermentation the tappers place small chips of coral rock in the pots. They imagine that this prevents fermentation but in fact it does not. The people, however, drink the toddy in the morning before fermentation has proceeded far. From the sweet toddy, jaggery and vinegar, for use on the island and also for export, are manufactured. The methods are crude and owing to the fact that slightly fermented toddy is used the jaggery produced does not harden like the jagery manufactured on the mainland but remains a viscous suggary substance and is exported in tins or in balls wrapped in leaves. It has a sweeter flavour than the mainland jaggery.

Topee making. Until a few years ago many of the Melacheries of Agathi used to go regularly to the coast where they remained during the fair weather making the characteristic Moplah embroidered cap. As the price of the more elaborate caps ranged up to Rs. 15 this was a very profitable undertaking. The islanders on account of their skill were in particular request for making the caps, but they have now almost entirely given up this occupation, though a few still make caps for the islanders themselves.

Agriculture Practically the only form of agriculture found on the islands is the cultivation of the coconut, but the methods adopted are crude and ignorant. No system of manuring is followed. In many places serious overplanting has been practised. The natural result is a decrease in the annual crop, of which the people are at last becoming aware.

On Androth, Agathi, Kavarathi and Kalpeni, in the tottams or āvals, excavations in the centre of the island made by the islanders in very ancient times, a little paddy, ragi, gram, sweet potatoes or yams is grown.

Rats are a serious pest of the coconut trees. They have become entirely arboreal in habit, live and breed in the tops of the trees and the coconuts seem to have become their only food. The rats exist in enormous numbers and eat and destroy an incalculable number of coconuts. The ground underneath the trees is littered, on all the islands, with rat-eaten nuts. The only remedy seems to be a systematic hunting of rats and destruction of nests, accompanied by careful protection from invasion of trees once cleared, but it is doubtful whether the indolent islanders will ever undertake the vigorous campaign that would be required to diminish the pest appreciably, if not to exterminate it.

Another common pest of the coconut is the Rhinoceros beetle (Olyctes rhinoceros) a large black beetle which bores into the heart of the crown and the bases of the leaf stalks. In doing so it injures the young rolled-up leaves which when unfolded are seen to be all cut and tattered. On the mainland the holes bored are infested by an even worse pest, the Red Weevil but this is not known to occur on the islands. The grub of the Rhinoceros beetle is found in manure heaps, fallen tree trunks, piles of rotten cadjans, or in any heaps of similar decomposing rubbish, and the most effective remedy for the pest is to burn all rubbish and rotten tree trunks.

Traders have been established on Minicoy for many years. **Trade.**
On the other islands petty traders have appeared only in recent years. The great bulk of the trade is, as already stated, still in the hands of the boat owners who deal through a few brokers on the coast. The petty traders charged such exorbitant prices that it was found necessary in 1920 to fix a price for coir.

The principal exports are coconuts, copra, coir, jaggery, cadjans and firewood, and the principal imports rice, salt, tobacco, cloths, condiments, cattle, kerosine oil, timber, tiles, earthenware, in fact all the necessities of life, for which the people are entirely dependent upon the mainland.

CHAPTER VI.

GAZETTEER.

Agathi.

The island of Agathi situated in latitude 10° 51′ 30″ N. and longitude 72° 28′ E., about 35 miles north-west of Kavarathi and 40 miles south-west of Ameni is the most westerly of the Laccadive group. The reef forms an ellipse 5 miles in length by 3 miles broad. Along its eastern arc and lying slightly north-east and south-west is the island itself, slightly over 3½ miles long and 1,000 yards wide at its broadest point. The southern portion consists of a long narrow strip almost 2 miles long and of an average breadth of about 100 yards. This narrow southern portion is overgrown with jungle and contains only scattered coconut trees. The remainder of the island is thickly planted with coconuts interspersed with bread fruit, and contains the scattered houses of the inhabitants. Agathi is remarkable in that it possesses no storm beach; the eastern shore is composed only of sand, rising from the level of the reef flat, which is well exposed at low tides. To the south, separated from the main island by a narrow channel is the small uninhabited island of Kalpitti, fringed with dense undergrowth and containing only a few coconut trees in the centre. The area of Agathi is about 688 acres and of Kalpitti about 28 acres. Enclosed between the island and the reef on the west is the lagoon, the finest to be found among the inhabited islands. There are two entrances into the lagoon navigable by the island vessels, one situated close in-shore at the north-west end of the island and the other on the western side of the lagoon. The former is that ordinarily used by island vessels. It has a depth of about 7 feet of water at high tide. There is a very good anchorage for steamers just off it at a distance of about 1½ miles. The lagoon is nearly free from coral rocks and its navigation is easy.

Agathi is the hottest of the inhabited islands. The men construct small sleeping boxes of cadjans on the shore where they sleep during the hot weather months. The soil is unfertile. An attempt was evidently made in earlier times to construct a tottam, land artificially excavated so as to contain moisture for the cultivation of paddy and cereals, but the attempt was not very successful. A sort of bean (payar) is grown and also sweet potatoes, plantains and a few betel vines.

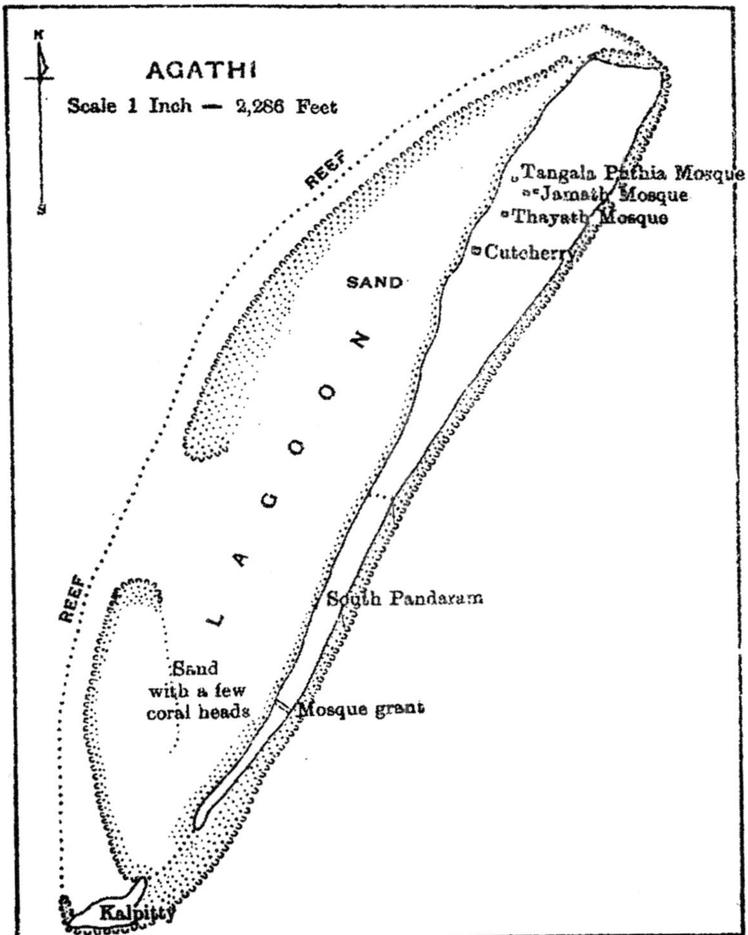

Reg. No. 504/12

Copies 512

Helio-Zinco., Survey Office, Madras.
1924.

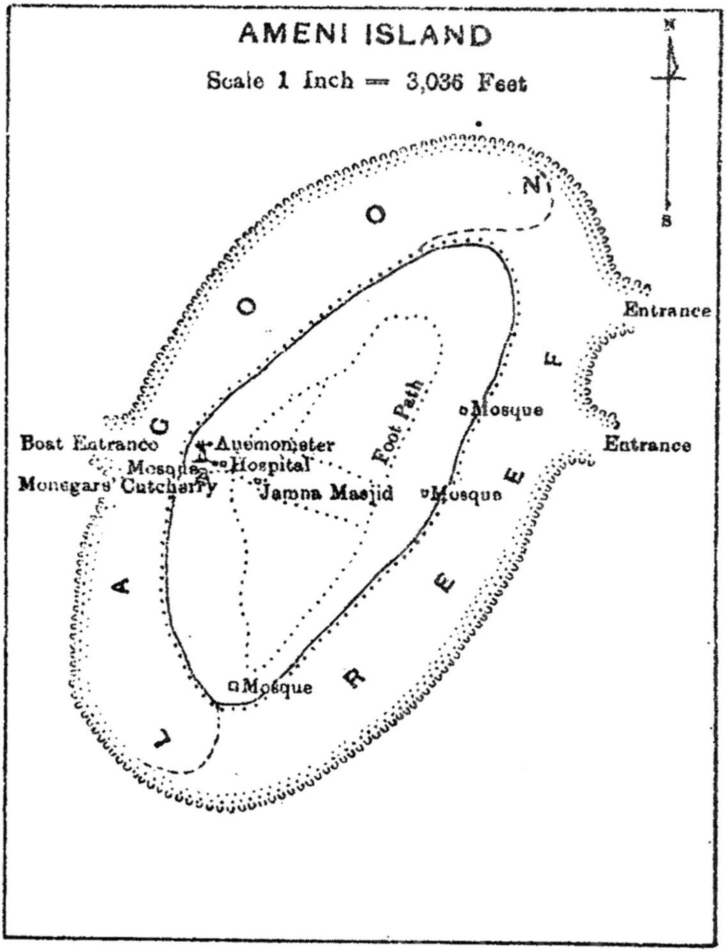

Reg. No. 504
11
Copies 512

Helio-Zinco., Survey Office, Madras.
1924.

The population in 1920 was 1,051 of whom 20 per cent are Koyas, 30 per cent Malmies and 50 per cent Melacheries. The houses are scattered through the northern portion of the island. They are built of thin slabs of limestone quarried from the beds of limestone found beneath the sandy soil, each slab being 2 or 3 feet in length, 2 feet wide and 3 to 4 inches thick. The houses contain a number of small rooms, each opening off the other and all dark and ill-ventilated. There is a verandah in front. The roof is made of cadjans. Only mosques have tiled roofs. The houses on Agathi are on the whole cleaner and better than on some of the other islands.

A new cutcherry was built in 1916 on the site of the old one. Near it lies an old ship's anchor said to be of 17th century pattern, but nothing is known of its history.

On the horizon to the northwards can be seen the coconut trees on Bangaram, Tinnakara and Parli.

The Pandaram lands on Agathi consist of the southern uninhabited portion of the island, which has been leased on cowle, and some scattered plots in the rest of the island.

On the southern face of Kalpitti, the sea has eaten away the reef rock to form a small "cliff" 6 to 8 feet high, in the face of which the action of the waves has worn numbers of holes and caverns. One of these is still pointed out by the islanders as the "Kunhi Bi para" the cave where a woman, the last surviving member of the Valiya Illam family, took refuge from a kavarcha carried out under the Beebee's orders about the close of the 18th century. The family as the result of the kavarcha was exterminated and its property either confiscated or destroyed.

Ameni (sometimes incorrectly spelt Amini) in latitude 11° 5′ N. and longitude 72° 45′ E. about 190 miles south-west from Mangalore is the principal island of the South Kanara group, and the headquarters of the Monegar and Sub-Assistant Surgeon. The island, which is about two miles long by over a mile wide with an area of 622 acres, almost completely fills the interior of the ring reef and only a very small lagoon is left on the western side. The beach on all sides is free from any bank of coral debris. There is a very conspicuous formation of beach sandstone on both eastern and western beaches. There are good anchorages off the reef on the west and four main boat entrances on the western side. The surface of the island is very even and in no place is more than 10 feet above sea level. In earlier times the centre was occupied by a tottam or kat for growing paddy and food grains, but this can never have been dug out to the depth Ameni.

found in the tottams on the Malabar islands and it has long since been filled in and almost completely planted up with coconut trees.

Sir W. Robinson in 1845 described the "tot" as occupying an extent of 55 acres in the centre of the island and stated that an unplanted strip of land some 200 yards broad existed along the western and southern shores, walled off for grazing from the rest of the island. This strip has long since been fully planted up. There is now no unoccupied land on the island. There are no Pandaram lands on the island. But there are a few Government trees, planted by previous Monegars and now either held by the nadpal as a service inam or granted free of rent to destitute persons.

The houses of the people are scattered all over the island. They are constructed like those on Agathi of slabs of coral limestone.

The cutcherry is a small two-roomed building with a porch, situated about 150 yards from the sea, near the middle of the western face of the island. Close beside it on the south are the Monegar's quarters while a little distance to the east are the dispensary, the Sub-Assistant Surgeon's quarters, the school, and the Meteorological Station. On the sea shore opposite the Cutcherry is a raised stone platform with a flight of steps leading down to the beach and mounted on the platform are two old cannons said to have been taken from the "Mahomed," a pilgrim ship wrecked at Ameni in 1854. The Portuguese had a fort on this island, all traces of which have now vanished. It was situated just north of the Cutcherry. Its foundations were dug up and used for building purposes within living memory. The Portuguese were poisoned as a result of a conspiracy hatched in the mosque still known as the Pambupalli.

The island is the most populous of the South Kanara group, the population in 1920 being 2,148. There are a few rich families but the majority of the people are poor and there seem to be more utterly destitute persons and destitute mainlanders on this island than on any other.

There are the usual three public mosques. The Jamath mosque is a large building constructed some 40 years ago mainly by the exertions of the then Monegar Mohamed Suleiman, who held office for nearly 25 years. On occasions of drought it is customary for all the islanders to join to rethatch the Nercha Palli and it is believed that this will bring the desired rain.

Clearly visible to the north, some 6 miles away, lies Kadamath. The Ameni islanders in early times claimed a

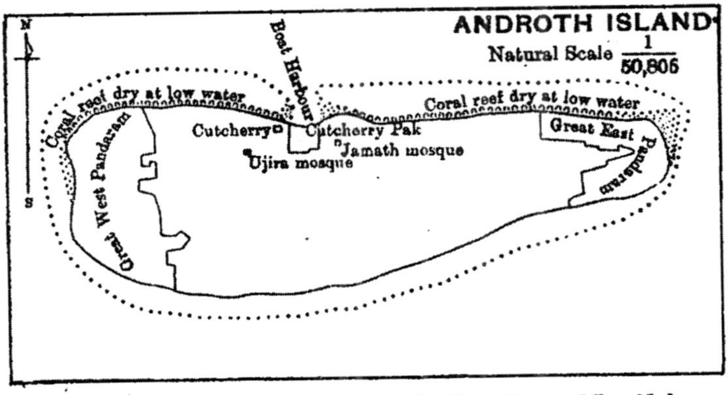

Reg. No. 504/10

Copies 512

Helio-Zinco., Survey Office, Madras.
1924.

certain control over Kadamath and refused to allow settlers there to hold trees of their own or to build their own odams. Even now the rich Ameni families own all the trees on the southern portion of Kadamath and Ameni Muktessors claim the right to sit in Cutcherry at Kadamath while the Kadamath Muppans stand.

The island is divided into four Cheries, Pallicheri in the south, Parakara in the east, Edanem to the north and Kodacheri to the west. There is one Kavalkar for each Cheri, but otherwise these old divisions appear to have lost all significance.

Androth in latitude 10° 48′ N. and longitude 73° 57′ E. lies about 123 miles from Calicut. Its greatest length is about 3 miles, its greatest breadth 1¼ miles and its area 1,067 acres. The island is remarkable among the Laccadives in that it occupies the whole interior of the atoll, leaving no lagoon, and also in that its longest axis lies east and west instead of north and south. Round the whole island, except at the north-east extremity, the reef flat is exposed at low tide. It is broader on the southern than on the northern face. At the eastern end of the southern face, a conglomerate, which appears to be continous with that of the reef, rises 5 to 6 feet above the level of the reef flat and passes under the sand forming the island; it appears to be continued into the layer of sandstone which everywhere lies beneath the sand. On the western side there is a small boat harbour. The harbour itself is slowly silting up and the entrance is being blocked up by the growth of coral. The entrance was once successfully opened up by blasting in 1909. Round the harbour are built the big sheds for housing the odams. Although all the available space has been utilised, there still is not enough room for sheds for all the odams. The remainder have to be thatched over roughly in the slip-ways in front of the odam sheds. This necessitates launching them each time before the odam in the shed behind can be launched. There is another smaller harbour about ¼ mile to the north where sites for odam sheds are now being taken up in order to avoid the present inconvenience. Androth.

About 150 yards south of the boat harbour is the new cutcherry, finished in 1919, by far the best built and most comfortable of all the cutcherries on the islands. The old cutcherry was a small dark building, badly situated behind the boat sheds. The new Cutcherry was built by the islanders themselves and presented to Government free of cost.

Just behind the boat sheds is the Jamath mosque, a big ugly tiled building but regarded with particular veneration as containing the tomb of the saint who converted the islands. A little south of the Cutcherry is the Ujira mosque and beside it, remarkable among island buildings in possessing an octagonal tower, is the tomb of Mohamed Kasim of the Sheikhindevittil family, third in descent from the original Sheikh, whose memory is still greatly revered on the islands.

The surface of the island is naturally level. In former times a large "tottam" has been excavated in the centre of the island and the sandy soil dug out forms mounds and hillocks all round it. In the tottam, which is divided up by bunds like a paddy flat on the mainland, are grown dry grains, ragi, varagu, millet, and sweet potatoes. The sides of the tottam are covered with a luxuriant growth of ferns. The soil on this island is richer than that of any other in the Malabar group: coconuts, bread fruit trees, plantains and betel vines grow well and a few areca palms and limes are to be found.

The Pandaram lands comprise about one-fourth of the area of the island. The largest blocks are the East and West Valiya Pandarams. The remainder are scattered among the holdings of the islanders. The East and West Pandarams represent waste land, originally belonging to the Bibi, granted on lease or cowle to the islanders. The other lands appear to have been acquired chiefly by escheat and confiscation. All are now leased out on the cowle system.

The population in 1920 was 2,492 of whom about 45 per cent are Koyas, 15 per cent Mālmis and 40 per cent Melacheries. The upper classes are perhaps richer than those of the other islands and greatly affect rich robes and waistcoats of silk or velvet for ceremonial occasions.

The island is divided into four Cheries, Edacheri on the north, Chemacheri on the south, Kicheri to the east and Mecheri to the west, but these divisions have now no political significance.

The most important event in the history of Androth was the great storm of 1847 which devastated the island. The population before the storm was 2,576. An unknown number of people perished in the storm itself. Large numbers of the survivors migrated to other islands to seek subsistence and were eventually settled upon Pandaram lands there by Sir W. Robinson. Those left upon the island numbered only 900. The coconut trees on the island were almost completely destroyed.

A school was first started on this island in 1878 and continued to be maintained with varying fortune until 1920,

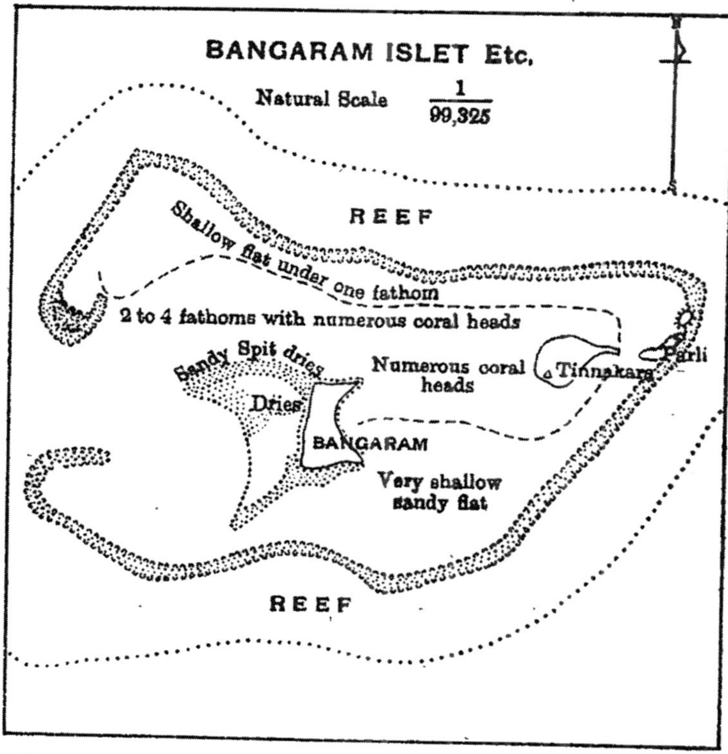

Reg. No. $\frac{504}{9}$

Copies 512

Helio-Zinco., Survey Office, Madras.
1924.

when it was closed for want of a teacher. It was reopened in 1921 a now has a strength of over 100.

A dispensary was maintained here between 1900 and 1905 but the people were at that time hardly alive to the benefit of European medical treatment and the dispensary was so little resorted to that it was decided to close it.

Bangaram, Tinnakara and Parli.

These are three uninhabited islands enclosed within one reef about 5 miles north of Agathi. Bangaram is 115 acres in extent, Tinnakara 76¾ acres and Parli 10 acres. They lie down the long axis of the lagoon and do not touch the reef except at the northern end. They are in fact sand banks in the middle of the lagoon; this probably accounts for the absence of the lime stone layer upon these islands. Parli is still little more than a sandbank and contains only a few trees, but the other two islands seem to be extremely fertile. They are covered with a dense impenetrable jungle of screw pine. Coconuts grow well and it is only the impossibility of finding fresh water that has prevented the islands from being occupied. An attempt by Sir W. Robinson in 1847 to colonise them failed for this reason. These islands strike the visitor as being even hotter than Agathi. Bangaram is the southernmost of the three islands; Tinnakara lies about 1½ miles north of it and Parli is about 400 yards north of Tinnakara and connected with it except during the monsoon by a strip of sand. The reef, which has several feet of water over it even at low tide, encloses a magnificent lagoon, about 6 miles long by 3½ miles wide. Except near Tinnakara where at low tide there are only a few inches of water for some distance from the shore, the lagoon is very deep, with here and there great bosses and plateaux of coral growing up to the surface. The fishing in the lagoon is very good. The islands are much frequented by men from the other islands who come to fish and to cut brush-wood.

These islands were originally the property of the people of Agathi. They were confiscated by the Bibi about 1764 as a punishment for the murder of an obnoxious accountant. At first, free use of the shoal was allowed to the Agathi islanders and a charge of Rs. 400 was made upon them for it but subsequently the islands strictly preserved and no one was allowed to visit them except when the Bibi's Kariyakar went to gather the nuts. Once or twice a year the whole population of Agathis, men, women and children, were required to go to the islands and gather cowries for the Pandaram. The right of plucking nuts is now auctioned for five years at a time and the lease is saddled with the condition that a specified number of seedlings must be planted during the period of the lease. The lease was sold in 1920 for Rs. 2,745 per annum.

Bitra. Bitra in latitude 11° 33′ N. and longitude 72° 6′ E. some 43 miles north-west of Ameni and 30 miles from Chetlat is the most northerly of the Laccadive islands. Although several attempts have been made to settle families from the other islands upon it, it still remains uninhabited. It is about 1,150 yards long by 200 yards broad at the widest point and some 26 acres in extent. It is situated at the north-east corner of the reef. The island is extending gradually on the northern shore and along the eastern arc of the reef, but is at the same time being washed away to the south inside the lagoon. Its whole shape appears to have altered very considerably within the last fifty years. The reef encloses a magnificant lagoon, 7 miles long by 3 miles wide.

There are about 1,200 coconut trees on the island of which some 350 are in bearing. Excluding 75 trees set apart for the use of pilgrims visiting the island, the remainder are leased out for three years at a time, with a condition requiring the planting of a certain number of young trees each year. A small shrine contains the tomb of a Pir or saint to which pilgrimages are frequently made from the other islands.

Sir W. Robinson records that up to about the year 1835 the island was the breeding ground of countless numbers of sea-birds and that the islanders used to collect their eggs in very large quantities for food, but that about that year the birds suddenly ceased to come. They have never been known to breed on the island since.

Chetlat. Chetlat in latitude 11° 44′ N. and longitude 72° 45′ E. some 35 miles almost due north of Ameni is a long narrow island about 1 mile 1,150 yards long by 650 yards wide at the broadest point, 255 acres in extent, and occupies the eastern arc of the attol. Along the whole eastern side of the island is a wide belt of coral debris, evidently the result of some severe storm. This belt broadens out at the south till it covers the whole southern end of the island. The reef is more perfectly circular than is the case in the other islands. The lagoon is about ¾ mile wide. The best anchorage for steamers is off the southern end of the reef.

The soil of the island is poor and the yield of the coconut trees in consequence not so good as on the other islands. The people themselves, all Melacheries, are poor but at the same time the thriftiest and most hard-working of all the islanders. The island is a model of neatness; no rubbish or debris will be found lying about; every fallen nut and every fallen coconut leaf is utilized for some purpose. The result

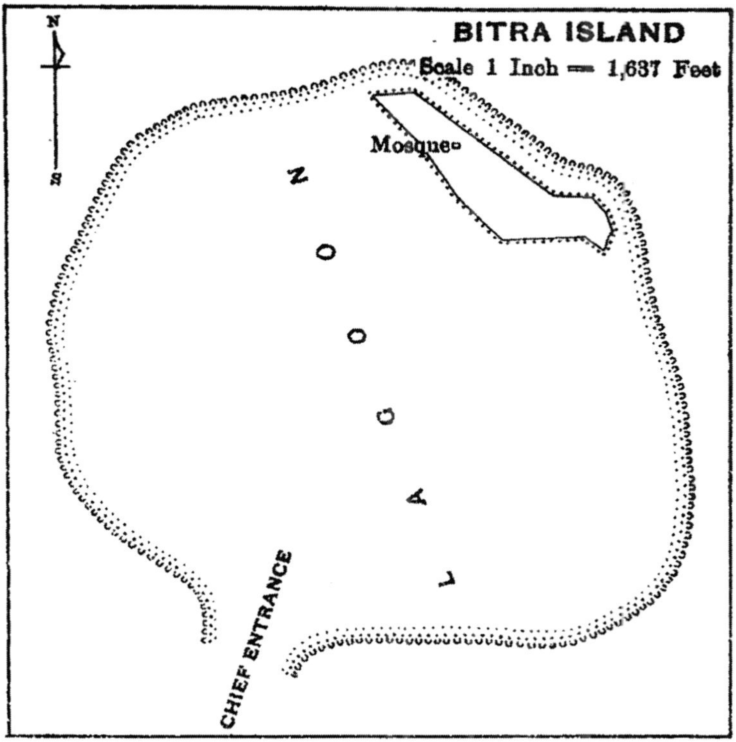

Reg. No. 504/8

Helio-Zinco., Survey Office, Madras. 1924.

Copies 512

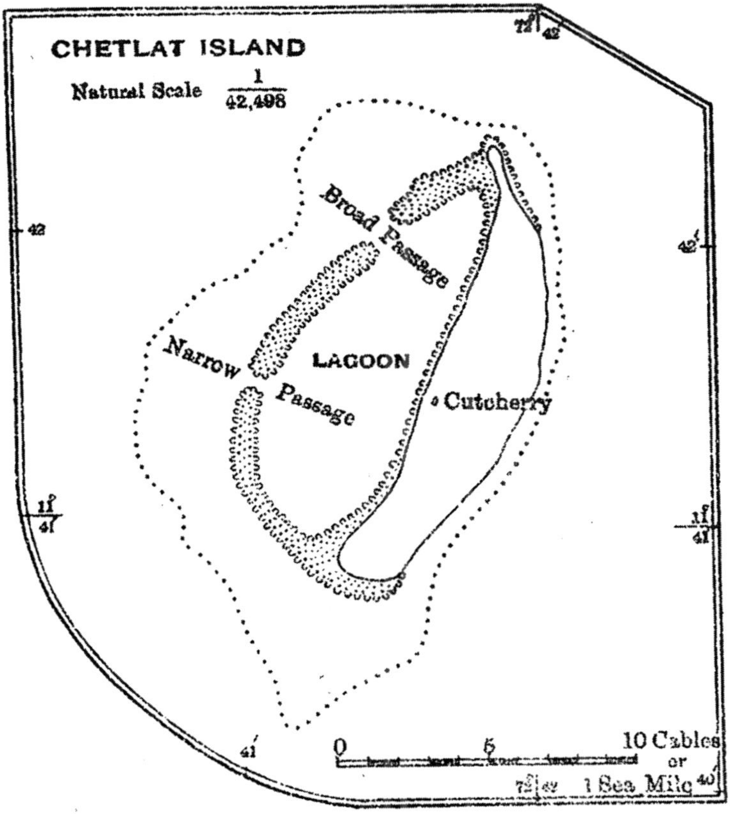

Reg. No. 504/7

Copies 512

Helio-Zinco., Survey Office, Madras. 1924.

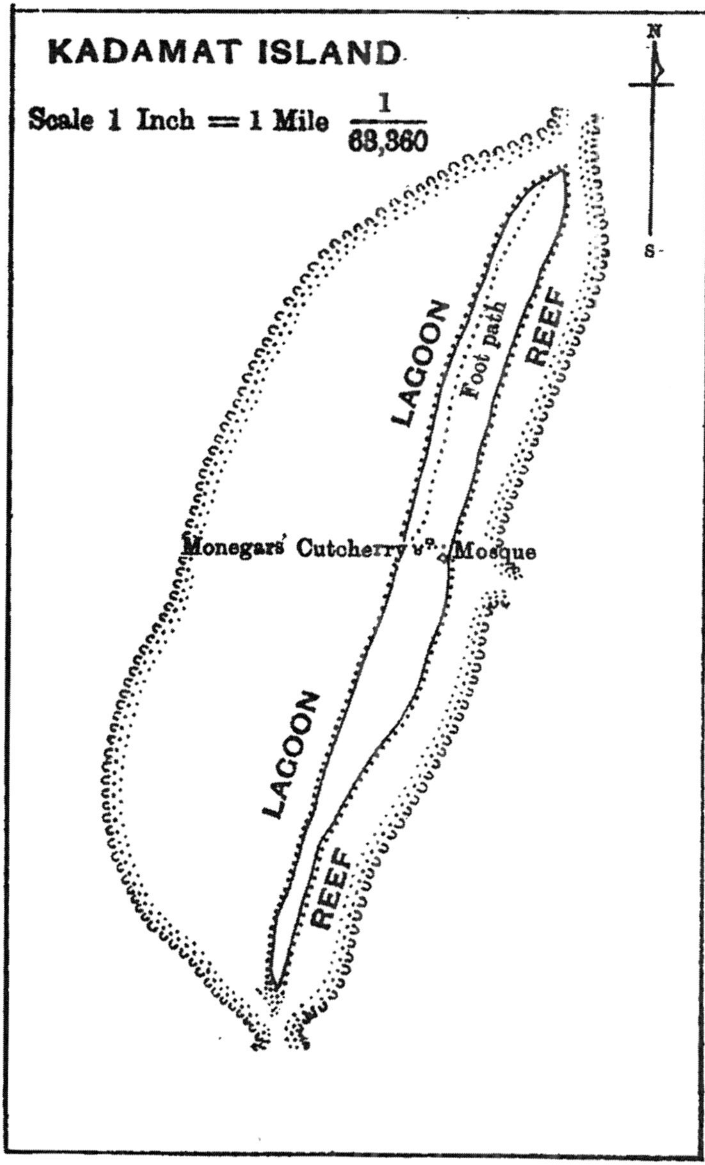

Reg. No. 504/6

Copies 512

Helio-Zinco., Survey Office, Madras.
1924.

of this industry is shown in the large exports of plaited cadjans to the mainland. The average Chetlat coir is equal to first-class coir of the other islands and Chetlat first-class is considerably superior to any coir produced on any of the other islands with the exception of Minicoy.

The cutcherry is about half way down the western side of the island, near the shore. It is a small incommodious building. In the same part of the island are the scattered houses of the inhabitants, the northern and southern ends being uninhabited and not very fully planted with coconut trees. South of the cutcherry on the eastern side of the island is the tomb of Carpenter Primrose of the *Vizier*, wrecked on Cheriyapani in 1853, who died on Chetlat while waiting to be taken off. The roughly carved stone was erected by the crew of the "*General Simpson*" wrecked on Chetlat in 1863.

Kadamath, 6 miles north of Ameni, is 5 miles 150 yards long by 600 yards wide at the broadest point, situated along the eastern side of a magnificent lagoon 7½ miles long by 1½ miles wide. The eastern arc of the reef is exposed at low tide and forms a level platform stretching from the sea beach for about 100 yards. This being the more sheltered side than the lagoon beach the coir soaking is done in "pits" constructed on the reef platform. The main boat entrances are at the southern end of the reef. A high ridge of sand runs down the western side of the island. Kadamath.

The southern third of the island, which belongs to the people of Ameni, is uninhabited and until 30 or 40 years ago was covered with thick jungle and contained few coconut trees. It has now been fully planted. The few houses are scattered round the Cutcherry on the western side of the island about 2 miles from the southern end. Except for a few small huts the northern half of the island is uninhabited and portions still remain unplanted. It is less fertile than the southern half but is in possession of the Kadamath islanders themselves.

The people who are all Melacheries are very poor. Until about 1860 no one on the island owned trees of his own. All were tenants of the Ameni people who exercised a kind of suzerainty over the island and in fact claimed that it was their property. They had until that time refused to allow the Kadamath people to build coast-going boats of their own and the whole produce of the island had to be shipped in the Ameni odams. Every effort, however, was made by Government to break this tyranny and by 1880 the only rights remaining were the personal ones existing between tenant and landlord and the Ameni Khazi's religious jurisdiction over the Naib Khazi of Kadamath. It was not until 1869 that the Kadamath islanders succeeded in building three small coast-going boats.

In 1907 the Ameni Khazi's authority over the Kadamath Khazi began to be openly questioned. The dispute aroused bitter feeling on Kadamath and was the cause of almost the only criminal appeals that have ever been received from that island. The Ameni Khazi claimed that the Kadamath Khazi was and had always been his Naib or Deputy and that as such his approval was required to the appointment of Naib Khazi of Kadamath. The monegar decided the case in favour of the Ameni Khazi. His decision was confirmed in appeal by the inspecting officer in 1908 and by the Collector. The people, however, refused to accept this decision and in 1909 when the Ameni Khazi performed the Kutba in the Kadamath mosque, as being Principal Khazi of Kadamath, in accordance with the decision, the people refused to attend and the Kadamath Khazi resigned. The islanders then erected a cadjan mosque and appointed one of themselves to read the Kutba in it. The monegar prohibited this but several islanders disobeyed him and many more seemed inclined to set authority at defiance. Feeling ran very high for some years, but a satisfactory compromise has been arranged by which the Kadamath congregation makes, the selection but the candidate has to obtain the Ameni Khazi's approval before he is finally appointed by the Collector.

The lagoon provides excellent fishing and the Ameni islanders regularly resort to it for that purpose. At the date of Sir W. Robinson's visit (1845) they used also to come over and raise hakkal cultivation (ragi, cholam and Indian corn) during the monsoon, but by 1870 this practice had quite ceased.

Kalpeni. The island of Kalpeni lies about 44 miles almost due south of Androth in latitude 10° 7″ N. and longitude 73° 55″ E. It is the most southerly of the Laccadives proper. Besides the main island there are two small rocky islands to the south-west, Thilakkam and Pitti, separated from the main island and from each other by narrow channels a few yards wide, and about 1½ miles to the north but connected by the reef flat which is almost dry at low tide is a long narrow island, Cheriam. Before the storm of 1847, the main island extended northwards along the reef flat almost to Cheriam. All four islands are enclosed within the same ring reef which forms the eastern shore of Cheriam and Kalpeni and the south-western shore of Pitti and Thilakkam and encloses a magnificent lagoon over 7 miles in length and about 2½ miles broad. The

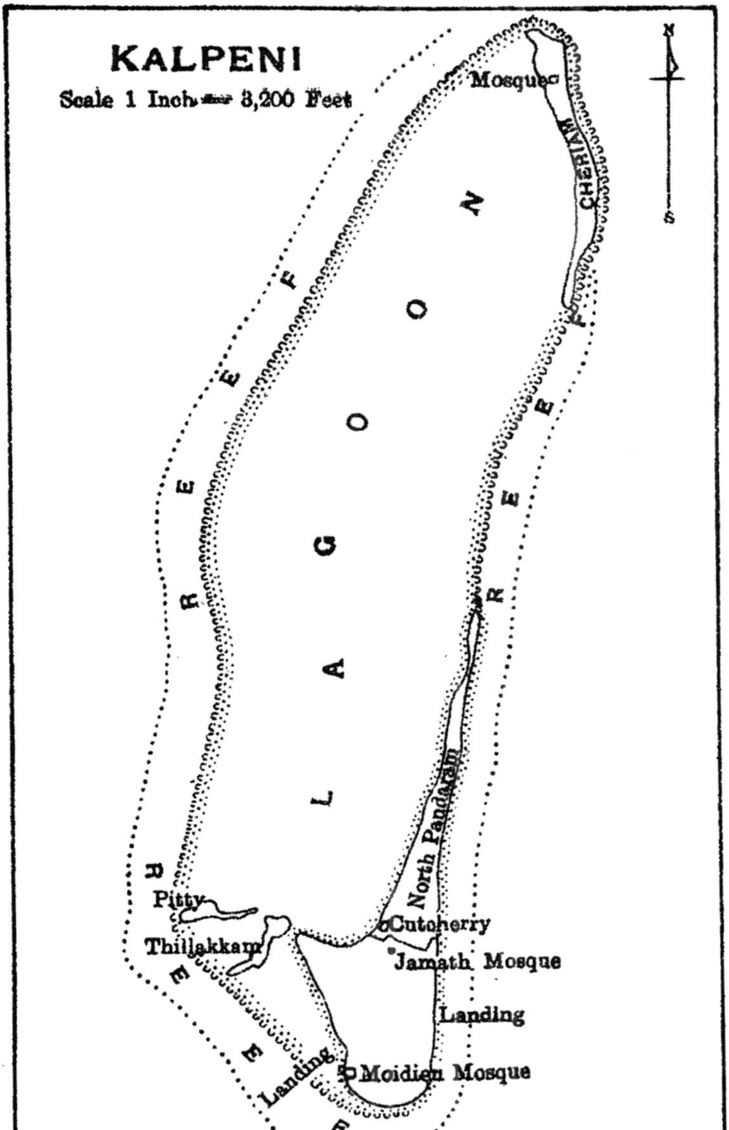

Reg. No. 504/5

Copies 512

Helio-Zinco., Survey Office, Madras.
1924.

two small islands on the south-west with the reef enclose between them and the main island a small lagoon through which a boat passage leads to the sea. The extreme length from the north point of Cheriam to the south point of Kalpeni is 7 miles and the greatest breadth about three-quarters of a mile. The total area of all four islands is 650 acres ; Kalpeni being 494 acres, Cheriam 130 acres, Thilakkam 12½ acres and Pitti 13½. The main island is about 3 miles long. The first mile from the north consists of a narrow strip of sand not more than 50 to 100 yards wide. The strip then suddenly widens out to about 400 yards and within a very short distance further to the south the island attains its maximum breadth. Only this broad southern portion of the island is inhabited. The houses are scattered through it at considerable distances apart. Cheriam is covered with a dense jungle of screw pine, killi and chonam. There are a few coconut trees on Cheriam which have been planted by islanders in fulfilment of vows made when detained by contrary winds or caught in storms and the nuts of these trees are used by any islanders coming to Cheriam. The existence of these trees made it impossible to grant any cowles for land on Cheriam, although there was a good demand for them, until 1922, when the scruples of the islanders were overcome and the whole island, with the exception of a small portion round a mosque, was parcelled out into approximately 2-acre plots and these were granted on cowle. Large quantities of brush-wood are cut on Cheriam and exported to Mangalore. The two smaller islands are well planted up.

A peculiar feature of Kalpeni is the huge storm bank of coral debris thrown up by the great storm of 1847 along the eastern and south-eastern shore. At the latter point this bank attains a height of some 12 feet and is perhaps 60 feet broad at the base; along the eastern shore it can still be traced inland for a distance of quite 100 yards. Another peculiarity is the absence of the sand-stone substratum found in all the other inhabited islands. The reef rock is strikingly exposed along the eastern side of the sandspit connecting the island with Cheriam. It slopes gently eastwards under the water and ends abruptly on its western face in a small "cliff" 4 or 5 feet above the sand which seems to indicate the previous margin of the lagoon before the deposition of the present sand bank. For about a mile at the north end of the island the lagoon shore is covered with much weathered boulders and the reef flat between the main island and Cheriam is even more thickly covered with them. These boulders were probably carried to their present position by the storm of 1847. A smaller cyclone early in December 1922 had cast up a smaller storm bank outside the earlier bank, 7 or 8 ft. high in parts and 20 to 30 yards wide, all along the eastern shore. This new bank extends northwards like a natural break water along the reef flat between the main island and Cheriam with only one gap and if it remains in its present position it seems likely that the island will again in course of time extend considerably to the northwards.

The soil of the main island is good in the central and southern portion, but the northern portion is mere sand. In the centre is a large tottam, consisting of low arable land, excavated by the islanders in former times, in which grains and a little coarse paddy, plantains and sweet potatoes, are grown. It has not been dug out so deep and has not the same charm of scenery as the tottam at Androth. The bread fruit grows well. There are a few areca palms, one tamarind and a few limes. Some betel vines are also cultivated, but on the whole the island does not strike the visitor as being so fertile as either Androth or Kavarathi.

The three smaller islands are covered with coral debris and are considerably less fertile than the main island.

There is one good boat passage through the reef near the north-western side, a considerable distance from the landing place and anchorage off the inhabited part of the island. There is, however, a passage for small boats through the reef into the little lagoon, which was blasted for the islanders in 1913. The anchorage for ships is just off the south-eastern point and there is a convenient landing place on the eastern shore about a mile from the southern end. This, however, cannot be used if the sea is rough.

The cutcherry is on the western shore exactly opposite the eastern landing place. There are the usual three public mosques, the Moidin Mosque being at the extreme southern end of the island, rather picturesquely situated upon the high ground formed by the storm beach and surrounded by walls of coral stone neatly built without mortar.

The houses, owingto the absence of sandstone, are built in manner peculiar to this island. Stakes formed of the midribs of the coconut leaf are driven into the ground in two rows about 6 inches apart and the two rows are tied together with withies. Sea worn coral stones from the beach are then packed in between the two rows of stakes as neatly as possible and plastered over on both sides. Sometimes the stakes are removed; often they are left standing. All the houses are enclosed with fences of cadjans.

The population in 1920 was 1,375 of whom 60% are Koyas perhaps 10% Malmies and the remainder Melacheries. The people are inferior in physique to the other islanders and are also the most ignorant and superstitious and by far the laziest. Even the simple task of conveying the saman of the Inspection party to and from the steamer is almost more than their energies are capable of. Nearly all the heavy work is done by the women and it is the women who have to carry the rice mudas from the shore to the houses when an odam comes in. In consequence of the laziness of the people the island is one of the most untidy. Fallen leaves and nuts lie littered everywhere.

The Pandaram lands occupy almost the whole of the northern portion of the island, from the Cutcherry northwards. There are some other scattered plots and one big block in the south: all were granted on cowle by Mr. Twigg in 1889. In 1885 all these lands were dense jungle and contained only scattered trees. There is now practically no jungle on the main island except a little at the extreme north end.

The island is divided into four Cheries, Vadakancheri, Tekkancheri, Kicheri and Mecheri.

The most notable event in Kalpeni history was the great storm of 1847. It commenced about 8 p.m. on 15th April, passed on to Androth which it reached between 12 and 2 a.m. on the 16th and finally reached Kiltan.

"The sea rose and flooded the whole island, but across the narrow part of the main island it seems to have had tremendous velocity. All the trees with the very soil, and between 50 and 60 houses were washed into the ocean with upwards of 200 persons, while along the whole length of the shore a flood of loose coral has been deposited over the island which will render a considerable tract quite unserviceable until it has decomposed and become soil. Across the broader parts of the islands the water was not so destructively rapid, but so complete was the inundation that the first impression of the islanders was that the whole shoal was sunk. The water filled the tottam with salt water, killing all vegetation and drowning many persons. It was in consequence last year quite waste. Over the eastern bank of the tottam a flood of loose coral stones was poured which has filled up and destroyed a part of this useful land. Many wells and tanks were filled with sand and stones and the fresh water in all of them was spoilt. The inundation was probably more destructive than the wind and has shaken the confidence of the people in the stability of the islands greatly.

"The storm lasted for about an hour in all its violence. Then a sudden lull came and the wind soon sprang up briskly from the westward and the flood subsided leaving the island in the most perfect state of desolation. Of the 348 houses standing before the storm, not one escaped. Many were so entirely washed away as scarcely to leave vestiges of their foundations. All were unroofed and otherwise damaged. All the mosques 29 in number were injured and nearly all of them at the time of Mr. Robinson's visit were lying in a state of ruin. The population of Kalpeni prior to the hurricane is reckoned at 1,642. Of these 246 were drowned or washed away during the storm. One hundred and twelve perished in the ensuing five months from famine or from the diseases engendered by unwholesome and insufficient food, 376 escaped to the coast, leaving in the island 908 of whom nearly four-fifths are women and children.

"The plantations in the island have been entirely destroyed. Out of upwards of 105,000 full-grown coconut trees, the number before the storm, only 768 are now standing. The other trees, bread fruit, banana, and betel-nut are likewise all lost." (Board's Proceedings, dated 2nd August 1849.)

The object of Sir W. Robinson's visit to the islands in 1847 was to enquire into the condition of the people after the storm and to devise methods for relieving the acute privations which it was known they were suffering. Numbers of refugees from Kalpeni were settled by him upon Pandaram lands in the other islands and large remissions of rents were granted for several years.

Kavarathi. This island lies in latitude 10° 34′ N. and longitude 72° 57′ E. Its length is about 3½ miles and its greatest breadth about ¾ mile. Its area is 865½ acres. It is 74 miles from Kalpeni and 35 from Agathi. The lagoon is about a mile wide. The main entrance is off the north-west point of the island and is marked on the west by a small pinnacle of rock about 6 feet high which appears to be a portion of the original reef left untouched when the remainder was cut down by sea action to its present level. There is a good anchorage for ships off the south end of the island. All coir is soaked in pits on the lagoon beach and the beach is in consequence dirtier than on any other island, being strewn with coir debris husks and sea weed. There is a conspicuous development of beach sandstone along the beach. The southern end of the island appears to have been at one time a separate island but is now connected with the main island by a narrow strip of land about 50 yards wide. On the sea side at this point and extending round into the lagoon is a high storm beach composed of bits of coral rock and coral debris. The ridges marking each successive storm that contributed to this beach can still be clearly traced.

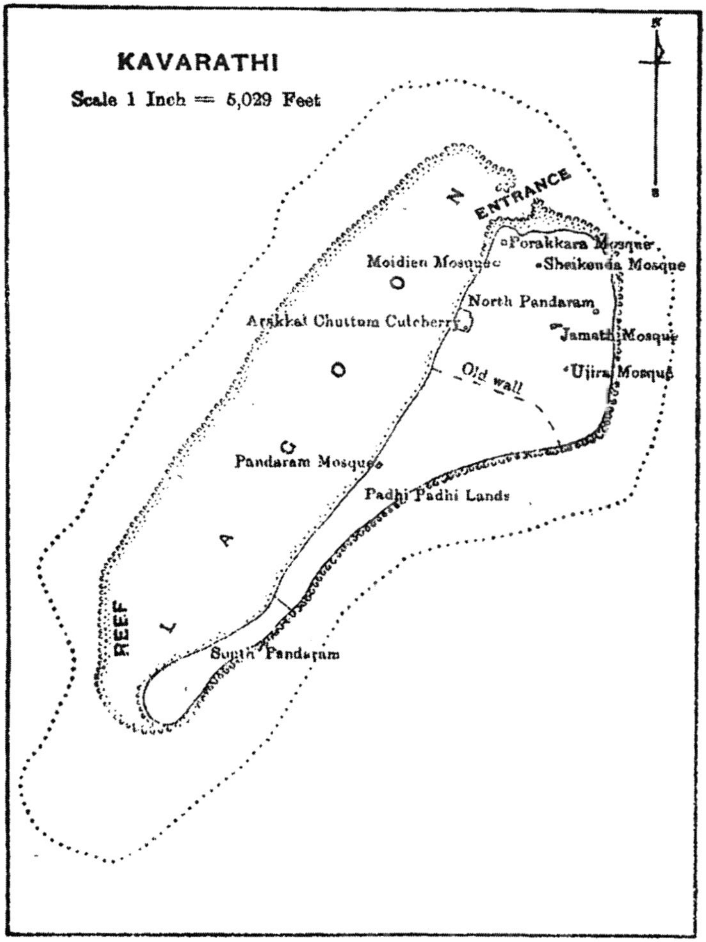

Reg. No. 504/4

Copies 512

Helio-Zinco., Survey Office, Madras.
1924.

At the northern end of the island is a small pond containing brackish water which appears to have been enclosed from the lagoon by the throwing up of a storm beach of coral debris during some storm.

There is no well-defined tottam now on this island. It is probably represented by a small valley in the centre. The only dry crop now cultivated at all extensively is payyar, a kind of bean, but yams, sweet potatoes, plantains and brinjals are grown in small quantities.

The population in 1920 was 1,606. Of these the Koyas form probably 10%, the Malmies 25% and the Melacheries 65%. This is therefore the most predominantly Melacheri island of the group and in fact the Koya and Malmi classes are believed to have been originally Melacheries who arrogated to themselves position and privileges in imitation of the Koya classes on the Tarwad islands. Class feeling is in consequence perhaps more bitter on this island than on any other. The Koyas not only deeply resent any encroachment upon their privileges but are always attempting to set up new prerogatives while the Melacheries who represent nearly two-thirds of the population find even their legitimate efforts to improve their condition hotly opposed by the higher classes. Feeling ran very high in the two or three years preceding the inspection of 1920 and culminated in widespread destruction of betel vines, which are mainly grown by the Malmi class, and several cases of incendiarism which included the cutcherry, burnt down in August 1920.

The island is divided into four Cheries; Mecheri on the north-west, Tekkecheri to the east with Porakecheri lying south of it and Pallicheri south of Mecheri. In Mecheri and along the western side the houses are ranged in rows along pathways almost like a village. In the rest of the island they are scattered. There are no houses in the southern half of the island which is all Pandaram land and was once separated from the inhabited portion by a wall. Under the Bibi's administration no islander was allowed to go south of the wall without a pass from the Bibi's kariyastan.

The cutcherry was a small incommodious building situated about 1½ miles from the northern end of the island. The only other Government building on the island is the small school about 100 yards north of the cutcherry. The mosques are better built than those on the other islands and many contain very beautifully carved pillars while in the grave yards are to be found headstones stained a delicate green or blue with Arabesque designs and Koranic texts well carved upon them. These islanders are noted for their skill in carving in both wood and stone. The Jamath mosque is a large building and possesses the largest tank of any mosque in the islands. The Ujira mosque, recently repaired and tiled possesses some particularly finely carved pillars and forms with the low arched sheds in front of it the most striking group of buildings upon the islands. The only other building that requires mention is a small private mosque dedicated to a Mussaliyar which has a picturesque tower with a large over-hanging thatched roof.

The Pandaram lands on the island have a complicated history. South of the wall in what was known as "the forbidden ground" no islander was allowed, under the Cannanore regime, to build a house, but quite a number obtained permission from the Karyastan to plant coconuts on condition that a share of the produce after deducting certain mamuls should go as rent to the Pandaram. These came to be known as the Padhi-Padhi lands from the system of sharing the produce. The arrangement, however, was a perpetual source of discord. The islanders were continually trying to secure more than their share of the produce, and even if the kariyastans insisted upon the Pandaram's share being fairly surrendered by the islanders they almost invariably embezzled as large a portion themselves as they safely could. The system made thieves of the islanders and rogues of the island officials. Mr. Winterbotham sought to abolish this arrangement in 1878 and introduce a system of cowles at a uniform rent of 10 pallams of first class coir per bearing tree or optionally in money at Rs. 1-8-0 per 100 pallams. Through some misunderstanding, however, his orders were not given effect to until Mr. Dumergue's visit in 1891 when cowles were issued upon the terms arranged by Mr. Winterbotham.

In addition to the Padhi-Padhi holdings in the "forbidden ground," there were other plantations planted and managed by the Kariyastans on behalf of the Cannanore family. Mr. Winterbotham in 1878 introduce a similar system of cowles for these also but at varying rates according to the condition of the plantations. He also granted cowles for the unplanted land.

Other Pandaram lands are the "Nattagathu" lands, i.e., those lying scattered through the inhabited portion of the island, north of the wall, and the "Idiyakkal" a large property escheated for reasons now unknown about 1840. These were also given on cowle by Mr. Winterbotham, the rent fixed being 15 pallams of coir per tree. Under the Cannanore administration, a claim peculiar to this island was

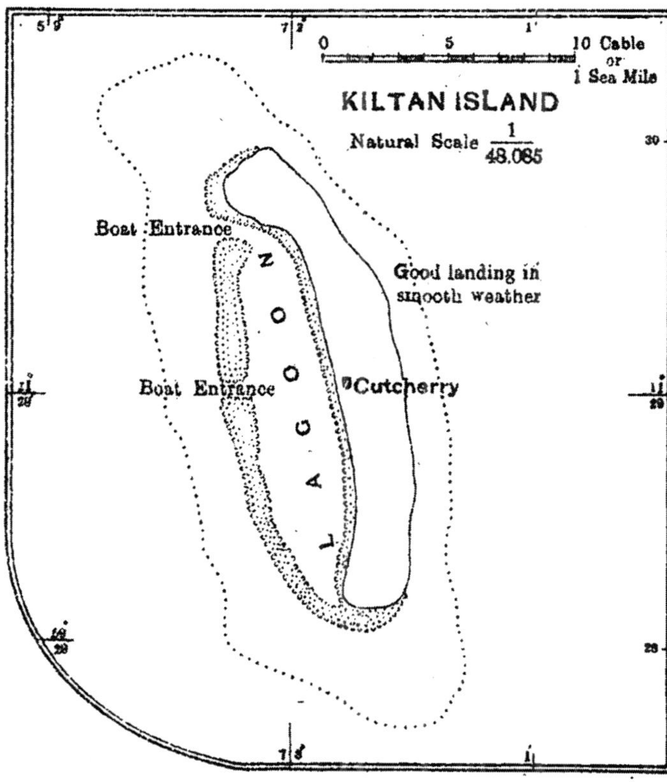

Reg No. 504/3

Copies 512

Helio-Zinco., Survey Office, Madras.
1924.

made to the land within 40 kols of the sea, and a tax, the Chuttu Karaima, was levied upon all trees growing in this belt. This tax was remitted by Mr. Logan in 1878 and the land within the belt was allowed to revert to the adjoining proprietors.

A violent storm burst upon the island on 5th February 1891, which did very considerable damage to the trees. Large remissions of rent upon the cowle lands were necessitated during the next few years.

Kiltan in Latitude 11° 28′ and Longitude 73° is situated some 30 miles north-east of Ameni. The island is 2 miles 100 yards long by about 650 yards wide at its broadest point and has an area of 397 acres. The lagoon is approximately the same length as the island and about 950 yards wide. There is a high storm beach of coral at both the northern and southern ends of the island, which continues for some distance along the eastern shore till it disappears near the centre of the island, leaving are open sandy beach. The northern storm beach is continued for some distance along the lagoon shore also, and was evidently caused by some heavy storm from the north. The island is steadily extending by accretion of sand on the lagoon side, so much so that the cutcherry which was once on the edge of the beach is now some 50 yards inland. There is a boat entrance through the reef off the northern point of the island but as the reef is left high and dry at low tide this canoply be used during high water. There is a good landing place on the sea beach on the eastern side of the island just opposite the cutcherry but this also is rather difficult at low water, although the reef in this position is not actually exposed. The coir soaking is all done in pits on the lagoon shore. Kiltan.

There is no unoccupied land on the island and no jungle. The people who are all Melacheries, though not so industrious as the Chetlat islanders, are better off and there are few destitute persons among them.

Minicoy is situated in Latitude 8° 7′ N. and Longitude 73° 19′ E. and is the most southerly of all the islands. It is distant about 243 miles from Calicut and 111 from Kalpeni. The island 1,120 acres in extent is crescent-shaped, 6⅛ miles long by about half a miles wide at the broadest point. For about two miles at the north, the island is little more than a ridge of sand and at some points only a few yards across. It then widens out and maintains fairly uniform breadth down to its southern point. To the south, separated by a channel about a quarter of a mile wide, is the small island of Viringilli, which is used by the islanders as a quarantine Minicoy.

station for small-pox patients and as a burial ground for those that die there. The lighthouse is about ½ mile from the southern point. About the middle of the island lies the village in which all the inhabitants live. One long path runs through it with several smaller ones intersecting it. The houses are built in rows along the paths. Each has a courtyard in front enclosed with neat cadjan walls and opening into the street by a curious swinging screen hung from the top to a horizontal pole above. The paths and open spaces are all neatly kept and the whole village gives a wonderfully pleasing effect of neatness and cleanness. There is a well in nearly every compound and in the open spaces. The wells are square in shape with plastered sides. Water is found within a short distance of the surface and is drawn by means of a coconut shell tied to a long stick. There are several fine bathing tanks in the village with plastered sides, steps leading down into the water, and parapets. Separate tanks are set apart for the women.

The village is divided into nine Attiris, each with its strip of foreshore. The Attiri clubs for men and women have been already described.

The population in 1920 was 3,093, of whom some 4 per cent are Malikhans, 6 per cent Malmis, 50 per cent Thakrus and 40 per cent Rāveris. Many of the men earn a livelihood as serangs and lascars on merchant vessels and are absent from the island for two or three years at a time. For this reason the women always predominate considerably over the men in numbers. A proposal to make Minicoy a special recruiting ground for the R.I.M. is under consideration.

A little over a mile north of the village is the leper settlement where the islanders segregate all persons declared by the Khazi to have leprosy. The population of the settlement varies from 10 to over 30. They receive a free dole of rice from Government and are supposed to be also provided for by their relations but most of them belong to the very poorest class and have practically to maintain themselves upon the Government ration.

The cutcherry is just beyond the village on the south. The islanders built and maintained for some years in front of it on the shore a small wooden jetty, but this has now disappeared. There are only two public mosques, the Jamath and the Moidin, but there are about 20 small private mosques.

The lagoon is a magnificent expanse of water about 6 miles long by 2 miles wide. It is very shallow towards the southern end of the island, and indeed at this point is almost dry at low water, but to the north and along the seaward side

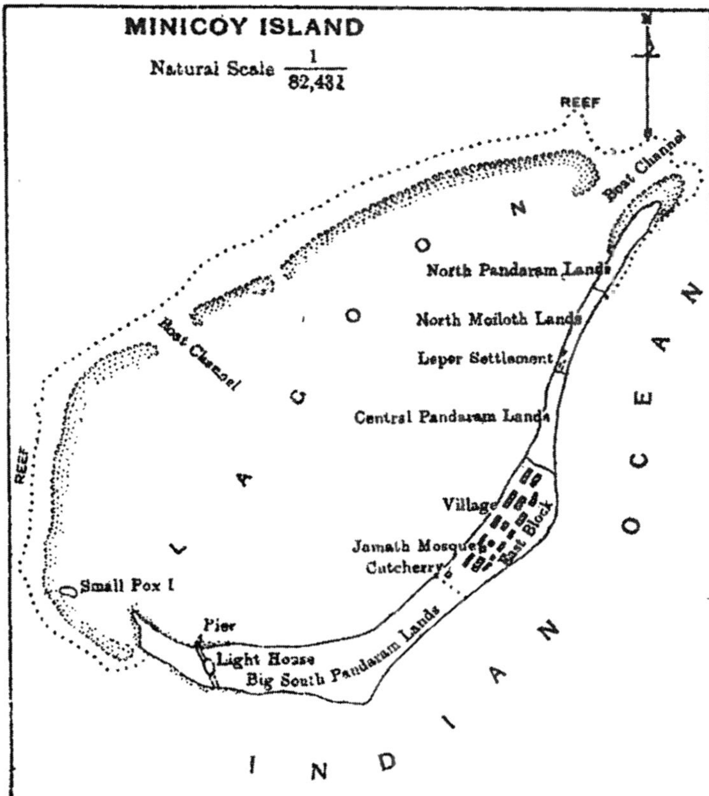

Reg. No. 504/2

Copies 512

Helio-Zinco., Survey Office, Madras.
1924.

it is deeper than any of the other lagoons and there is plenty of water close inshore for the large island brigs. Great bosses of coral rise here and there almost to the surface and make the navigation somewhat dangerous, but the people have marked out a safe channel to the passage through the reef by means of tripods made of long poles wedged into the coral bosses. A wooden beacon on the reef marks the one safe anchorage for ships, off the south-west end of the reef.

Unlike the other islands, Minicoy has never been subject to the coir monopoly. The chief sources of revenue were instead, under Cannanore rule, rent amounting to Rs. 780 paid by seven Malikhans for certain land held on Valiapattam, Attiri Pattam (sea shore rent) amounting to Rs. 264 paid by 112 islanders, the Allara, a poll tax, assessed by households by the Mukries of the Jamath mosque at the rate of 20 pounds coir for a man and 5 pounds for a woman per annum, Malikhans and all unmarried adults, being exempt, a tax on tappers at 45 Adubas of jaggery a year, a tax of 5 candies of rice a year on each large vessel and of 50 dried mas fish on each mas boat. In addition there was a cowry monopoly and the produce of the Pandaram lands, which comprised the whole island except the village site and a little private land around it. The Valiapattam in respect of any lands still so held, the Attiri pattam, the tapping tax and the poll tax are still paid, but the tax on boats and the cowry monopoly have been abolished. The system of managing the Pandaram lands continued until 1912 when Mr. Innes handed over to the islanders on a 30 years' lease the Great South Pandaram which extends from the cutcherry southwards and includes the greater portion of the island.

The Mas fishing, an industry peculiar to Minicoy, has already been mentioned. Coir, although not a monopoly, is extensively manufactured and is of considerably superior quality to that produced on the other islands.

There is no restriction upon trade such as results on the other islands from the Kudian system. The larger vessels voyage via Colombo even as far as Rangoon and Calcutta. This trade was until the late eighties of last century the monopoly of the richest man on the island, Dom Malikhan, who was famous throughout the Laccadives as "the Capithan." After his death his successors found it too expensive to maintain the longer voyages and his "brigs" were allowed to get into disrepair. Of recent years, however, the voyages have been revived again. One of his brigs has been bough and repaired by the islanders out of the proceeds of the

Great South Pandaram since it was handed over to their management, and is now being sailed by them as a co-operative enterprise to Calcutta.

The local trade on Minicoy which previously had also been Dom Malikhan's monopoly is now in the hands of some half a dozen Moplah traders from Cannanore who have set up shops and sell the ordinary bazaar commodities for coir, mas fish, or jaggery, and make enormous profits.

The health of the island is now good although at one time a particularly deadly form of malaria existed. In 1834 two of the East India Company's Naval officers who carried out the survey of Minicoy along with that of the Maldives, died of fever contracted on the island, and in 1883 Mr. Underwood and the members of his party, who made a long stay upon the island, suffered very severely. Of late years, however, malaria appears to have disappeared and the lighthouse keepers find Minicoy a healthy station. But mosquitos of the Culex variety occur in incredible numbers and constitute such a pest that even the islanders themselves are forced to sleep under mosquito curtains. Their breeding grounds appear to be, not the tanks and wells, but the coir pits and the rat eaten coconuts which fall from the trees and get filled with water during the monsoon. Every pit and every rat-eaten nut containing water will be found to be swarming with mosquito larvae, but a careful examination of the tanks and wells has so far failed to disclose any larvae in them.

The nine Attiris into which the village is divided are, from north to south :—

Bodu or Oyikolu.	Hanimagu or Ramadth.
Kudahi.	Raveri.
Punghilolu.	Bada.
Attodi.	Pallasseri.
Setivalu.	

The Varangies have the same names with the exception of those corresponding to Bada and Raveri which are known as Kolu and Digu Varangies.

Pitti.

Pitti is a small reef about 15 miles north-west of Kavarathi with a small sand-bank at its southern end. The Kavarathi islanders visit it for fishing and to collect the eggs of the numerous sea-birds which breed there between January and March. Major Alcock's description of his visit to the island during the breeding season has already been quoted (page 13).

The island has been leased to the Kavarathi Gumasthan since 1913 but up to 1920 he had been unable to get any

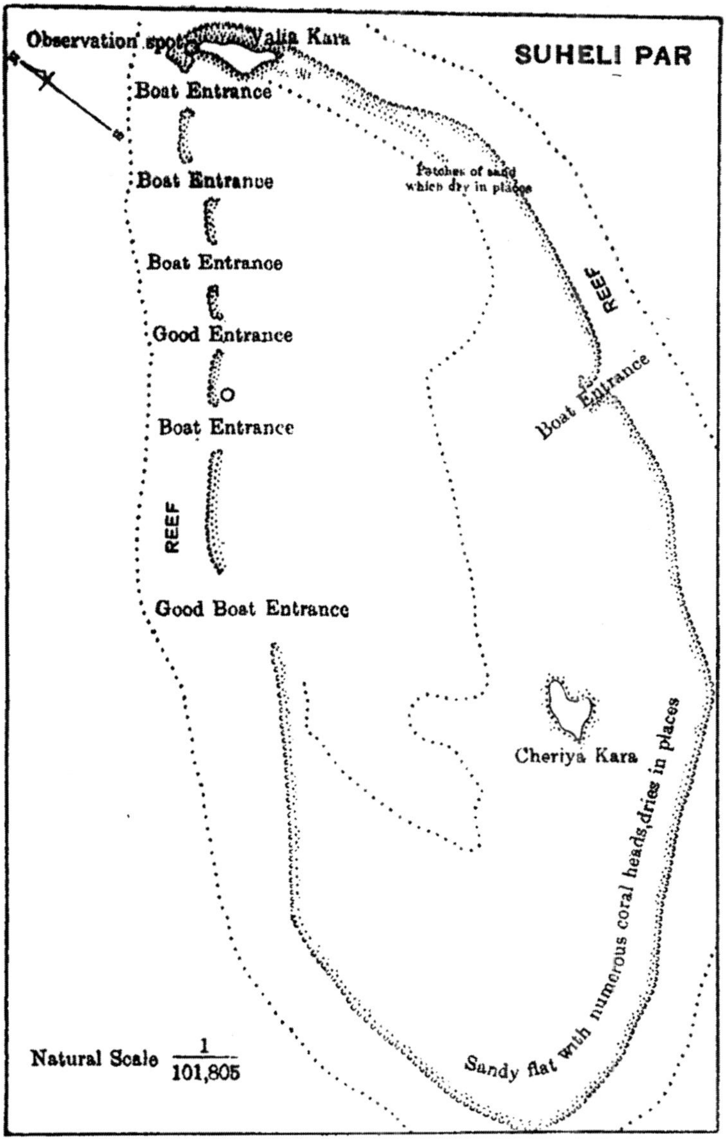

Reg. No. 504
1
Copies 512

Helio-Zinco., Survey Office, Madras
1924.

coconut plants to grow owing to the ravages of the crabs and the slanders visiting the reef.

Suheli or Suhelipar.

This reef lies about 40 miles south-west of Kavarathi and contains two small islands, about 6 miles apart, Valiyakara at the northern and Cheriyakara at the southern end, of which only the latter has been surveyed. It is 81¾ acres in extent. The northern island is probably a little larger. Both islands are very low, perhaps little more than 3 feet above high water mark. Both appear to be very fertile but the sandstone substratum is absent and good water consequently not plentiful. Both, like the islets in the Bangaram reef, are sand banks formed in the middle of the lagoon as do not touch the reef except at the nothern point of Valiyakara ; this fact seems to have some connexion with the absence of the sandstone. The northern island is completely overrun with jungle in which scattered coconut trees occur. Unlike the jungle on the other islands, it contains no screwpine but consists of large trees of various kinds, the commonest being the banian, over which ipomoeas and other creeping shrubs climb. At the eastern and western ends the jungle becomes smaller and is composed mainly of kanni. There are about 1,000 coconut trees on this island.

Cheriyakara is about ¾ mile long by ¼ mile wide. The lagoon in its immediate neighbourhood is very shallow especially on the south and east where large sandflats are left dry at low tide. Unlike the northern island it contains no big jungle but is covered in parts with cheruthalam and chonam bushes and in other parts with coarse long grass. There are about 3,000 coconut trees on the island. Near the centre of the island about 100 yards from the eastern shore there is an extensive shallow pond of stagnant water surrounded by a dense fringe of scrub.

Suheli is frequently visited by islanders from Kavarathi on account of the excellent fishing, and occasionally even by islanders from Agathi and Ameni. Fish, turtles, and the tortoise shell tortoise are abundant and in the days of the cowry monopoly large quantities of cowries used to be obtained. These fishing visits extend over several weeks. The visitors put up temporary sheds on the north-west shore of the southern island where large heaps of fish bones and other refuse bear witness to their occupation. The water obtainable is very brackish and for drinking purposes the islanders use the nuts of the neighbouring trees. The only buildings on the islands are a mosque of rude construction and the tomb of a Tangal much venerated by the islanders.

Many miracles are ascribed to him and it is customary to invoke his aid in storms or when delayed by adverse winds.

Suheli was formerly the private property of the Kavarathi islanders but was confiscated about 1765 in punishment for a suspected conspiracy and the murder of a Kariyakar of Kavarathi. It was managed by the Raja's agent at Kavarathi and is now in the charge the Kavarathi Amin. The right of plucking the nuts is now auctioned for five years at a time with a condition regarding the planting of fresh trees. The lease in 1920 fetched Rs. 1,505 per annum. But for the fact that Suheli became Pandaram property it would probably long ago have been colonised, for the water difficulty, on the southern island at least, seems to have been greatly exaggerated. Sir W. Robinson in 1848 attempted to found a colony of 200 emigrants from Kalpeni and Androth after the great storm, but the Bibi's Government naturally did not encourage the enterprise and it is hardly surprising that when the islands began to recover from the effects of the storm these people returned to their homes.

APPENDIX I.

Distances between the Laccadive Islands.

Calicut.
123 Androth.
175 58 Ameni.
207 99 43 Bitra.
178 76 35 30 Chetlat.
160 55 32 48 20 Kiltan.
207 85 33 43 56 60 Agathi.
187 64 35 67 68 62 31 Kavarathi.
210 89 62 90 95 91 44 29 Suhelipar.
143 47 81 123 111 95 96 67 76 Kalpeni.
240 158 168 203 204 187 160 136 118 114 Minicoy.

APPENDIX II.

POPULATION.

—	1831.	1845.	1848.	1869.	1876.	1880.	1891.	1902.	1911.	1920.
Minicoy ...	...	...	...	...	2,800	3,195	3,730	3,098	3,624	3,093
Kavarathi ...	...	...	2,060	1,784	2,016	1,979	2,126	1,953	1,606	1,461
Agathi ...	...	...	1,545	1,323	1,290	1,264	1,354	1,212	1,019	1,051
Kalpeni ...	...	...	1,642	986	1,029	1,137	1,317	1,513	1,643	1,375
Androth ...	...	...	2,576	...	2,629	2,599	3,320	2,441	2,708	2,492
Ameni ...	1,938	2,315	...	2,289	...	2,272	2,151	1,965	1,968	2,148
Kadmat ...	76	133	...	209	...	246	338	326	487	577
Kiltan ...	465	639	...	757	...	818	723	727	719	761
Chetlat ...	353	522	...	574	...	619	511	590	771	675

APPENDIX III.

STATEMENT OF RECEIPTS AND CHARGES FROM 1908 TO 1922.

AMINI-DIVIS.

Particulars. (1)	1908–09. (2)	1909–10. (3)	1910–11. (4)	1911–12. (5)	1912–13. (6)	1913–14. (7)	1914–15. (8)
Receipts.	CANDI. M. LB.	CANDI. M. LB.	CANDI. M. LB.	CANDI. M. LB.	CANDI. M. LB.	CANDI. M. LB.	CANDI. M. LB.
1. Quantity of coir sold ...	509 0 0	220 0 0	335 0 0	1,263 0 0	552 10 0	868 19 1	29 1 3
	RS. A. P.	RS. A. P.	RS. A. P.	RS. A. P.	RS. A. P.	RS. A. P.	RS. A. P.
2. Price realized	25,132 0 0	10,641 0 0	14,140 0 0	51,357 0 0	25,663 0 0	48,319 3 4	1,777 6 11
3. Other receipts	262 14 6	457 6 0	511 8 0	491 5 4	475 10 8	601 5 9	611 13 0
Total receipts ...	25,394 14 6	11,098 6 0	14,651 8 0	51,848 5 4	26,138 10 8	48,920 9 1	2,389 3 11
Charges.	CANDI. M. LB.	CANDI. M. LB.	CANDI. M. LB.	CANDI. M. LB.	CANDI. M. LB.	CANDI. M. LB.	CANDI. M. LB.
1. Quantity of coir purchased.	570 13 0	735 10 9	400 12 5	644 13 7	762 7 24	437 17 13	530 6 20
	RS. A. P.	RS. A. P.	RS. A. P.	RS. A. P.	RS. A. P.	RS. A. P.	RS. A. P.
2. Amount paid in cash ...	2,963 3 10	3,764 14 0	2,090 14 11	3,394 8 5	3,288 12 4	2,611 3 5	2,910 5 2
3. Amount paid in rice ...	22,245 7 0	24,294 14 2	12,193 5 3	21,329 1 8	23,538 7 9	20,882 11 3	22,431 4 0
Total payment for coir ...	25,208 10 10	28,059 12 2	14,284 4 2	24,723 10 1	26,827 4 1	23,493 14 8	25,341 9 2
4. Duty on salt supplied ...	851 4 0	730 12 0	905 4 0	798 8 0	797 12 0	976 4 0	910 12 0
5. Establishment charges ...	4,981 10 6	5,636 13 4	4,900 2 3	5,107 14 4	6,113 15 4	5,166 14 9	6,687 7 9
Total charges ...	31,041 9 4	34,427 5 6	20,089 10 5	30,630 0 5	33,738 15 5	29,637 1 5	32,939 12 11

APPENDIX III—*cont.*

STATEMENT OF RECEIPTS AND CHARGES FROM 1908 TO 1922—*cont.*

AMINI-DIVIS—*cont.*

Particulars.	1915–16. (9)	1916–17. (10)	1917–18. (11)	1918–19. (12)	1919–20. (13)	1920–21. (14)	1921–22. (15)
Receipts.	CANDI. M. LB.	CANDI. M. LB.	CANDI. M. LB.	CANDI. M. LB.	CANDI. M. LB.	CANDI. M. LB.	CANDI. M. LB.
1. Quantity of coir sold ...	1,411 3 4	406 10 0	91 12 11	694 10 0	949 10 0	730 11 17	935 0 0
	RS. A. P.	RS. A. P.	RS. A. P.	RS. A. P.	RS. A. P.	RS. A. P.	RS. A. P.
2. Price realized	67,377 1 2	18,292 8 1	5,711 9 6	23,752 8 0	43,482 8 0	34,296 11 7	54,892 8 0
3. Other receipts	805 13 5	793 15 7	582 2 3	419 0 0	1,632 9 6	1,303 1 6	1,174 14 4
Total receipts ...	68,182 14 7	19,086 7 8	6,293 11 9	24,171 8 0	45,115 1 6	35,599 13 1	56,067 6 4
Charges.	CANDI. M. LB.	CANDI. M. LB.	CANDI. M. LB.	CANDI. M. LB.	CANDI. M. LB.	CANDI. M. LB.	CANDI. M. LB.
1. Quantity of coir purchased.	879 19 22	560 7 16	616 13 11	604 11 7	784 10 4	727 16 20	521 7 6
	RS. A. P.	RS. A. P.	RS. A. P.	RS. A. P.	RS. A. P.	RS. A. P.	RS. A. P.
2. Amount paid in cash ...	4,306 8 9	2,912 5 10	3,202 5 7	3,070 0 9	4,071 7 11	3,826 13 8	2,702 2 3
3. Amount paid in rice ...	30,309 7 2	22,498 6 10	27,535 14 1	24,853 15 7	44,133 4 0	47,625 2 2	24,022 5 8
Total payment for coir ...	34,615 15 11	25,410 12 8	30,738 3 8	27,924 0 4	48,204 11 11	51,451 15 10	26,724 7 11
5. Duty on salt supplied ...	1,109 4 0	840 6 0	1,544 11 0	770 15 0	1,130 10 0	1,350 0 0	1,249 1 0
4. Establishment charges ...	6,968 8 10	6,442 5 10	6,126 15 5	6,070 12 8	7,392 7 2	8,416 6 9	8,985 10 3
Total charges ...	42,693 12 9	32,693 8 6	38,409 14 1	34,765 12 0	56,727 13 1	61,218 6 7	36,959 3 2

APPENDIX III—*cont.*

RECEIPTS AND CHARGES.

MALABAR ISLANDS.

Year.	Receipts.				Charges.					
	Quantity of coir sold.	Price realized.	Other receipts.	Total receipts.	Quantity of coir received.	Paid in cash.	Price paid in rice.	Total payment.	Establishment charges.	Total charges.
	CANDI.	RS.	RS.	RS.	CANDI.	RS.	RS.	RS.	RS.	RS.
1914-15 ...	766	40,441	1,0308	50,749	840	3,210	26,405	29,615	4,053	33,668
1915-16 ...	723	28,474	8,047	37,421	1,158	4,640	38,138	42,778	3,838	46,616
1916-17 ...	1,685	70,366	10,149	80,515	1,026	4,243	35,988	40,231	4,397	44,628
1917-18 ...	628	35,087	12,238	47,325	965	3,858	33,141	36,999	4,004	41,003
1918-19 ...	1,291	43,287	12,401	55,688	1,179	4,731	45,304	50,035	4,411	54,446
1919-20 ...	1,328	68,514	12,014	80,528	966	3,598	47,603	51,201	4,314	55,515
Total ...	6,421	2,86,169	66,057	3,52,226	6,134	24,280	2,26,579	2,50,859	25,017	2,75,876
Average ...	1,070	47,695	11,010	58,704	1,022	4,047	37,763	41,810	4,170	45,979

APPENDIX IV.

INSPECTING OFFICERS.

Name of officers.	Designation.	Date of visit.	Remarks.
MALABAR LACCADIVES AND MINICOY.			
		YEAR.	
1. Lieut. Bentley	...	1795	
2. Mr. (Sir) W. Robinson.	Head Assistant Collector.	1847	
3. " E. C. F. Thomas ...	Special Assistant Collector.	1856	
4. " E. C. F. Thomas ...	...	1858	
5. " W. Logan	Sub-Collector ...	1869	
6. " J. B. Spedding ...	Do. ...	1873	
7. " H. M. Winterbotham.	Special Assistant Collector.	1876	
8. " H. M. Winterbotham.	Do.	1877-78	
9. " V. A. Brodie ...	Do.	1880	
10. " W. G. Underwood.	Do.	1881-82	
11. " A. C. Tate ...	Do.	1884	
12. " G. W. Dance ...	Head Assistant Collector.	1884-85	

APPENDIX IV—*cont.*

INSPECTING OFFICERS—*cont.*

Name of officers.	Designation.	Date of visit.	Remarks.
MALABAR LACCADIVES AND MINICOY—*cont.*		YEAR.	
13. Mr. W. Logan	Collector ...	1887	
14. „ G. W. Dance ...	Head Assistant Collector.		
15. „ J. Twigg	Sub-Collector ...	1889	
16. „ W. Dumergue ...	Collector ...	1891	
17. „ Batten	Special Assistant Collector.	1892	
18. „ J. Hewetson ...	Collector ...	1895-96	
19. „ R. F. Austin ...	Head Assistant Collector.	1899	
20. „ G. H. B. Jackson ...	Do.	1902	
21. „ C. W. E. Cotton ...	Do.	1904	
22. „ C. W. E. Cotton ...	Do.	1905	
23. „ E. F. Thomas ...	Do.	1906	
24. „ J. K. Lancashire ...	Do.	1907	
25. „ R. H. Ellis	Special Assistant Collector.	1908	
26. „ R. H. Ellis... ...	Do.	1909	Inspected the South Kanara group also.
27. „ W. A. Doig ...	Sub-Collector ...	1912	
28. „ W. Rabjohns ...	Do. ...	1913	
29. „ F. B. Evans ...	Collector ...	1916	Only Minicoy and Androth.
30. „ R. H. Ellis ...	Do. ...	1920	Inspected the South Kanara group also.
31. „ R. H. Ellis ...	Do. ...	1922-23	
SOUTH KANARA ISLANDS.			
1. Mr. (Sir) W. Robinson.	Assistant Collector.	1844-45	
2. „ E. C. G. Sewell ...	Do.	Dec. 1865 to Jan. 1866.	
3. „ F. E. Hall	Do.	1869	
4. „ G. Stokes	Do.	1873	
5. „ H. Bradley... ...	Do.	1880	
6. „ Shujat Ali	Head Assistant Collector.	1886	
7. „ D. W. G. Cowie ...	Do.	1891	
8. „ A. M. Slight ...	Do.	1892	
9. „ M. E. Couchman ...	Assistant Collector.	1895	
10. „ A. F. G. Moscardi.	Do.	1899	
11. „ A. F. G. Moscardi.	Head Assistant Collector.	1902	
12. „ W. A. Doig ...	Assistant Collector.	1904	
13. „ J. K. Lancashire ...	Head Assistant Collector.	1956	
14. „ J. K. Lancashire ..	Do.	1906	
15. „ W. A. Doig ...	Do.	1907	
16. „ J. F. Hall	Do.	1908	

APPENDIX V.

ANCHORAGES.

Agathi	N. Tan. Agathi S. 74½° W. W. Tan. in transit with W. Tan. of Kalpitti S. 31½° W. in 4½ fathoms.
Ameni	Left Tan. Kadamath N. 31° E. Left Tan. Ameni N. 64° E. Cutcherry S. 74° E. in 3¾ fathoms.
Androth	Mosque among boat sheds round harbour S. 18° E. at 2·8 cables in 4 fathoms.
Bangaram	Right Tan. Tinnakera N. 86° E. Right Tan. Bangaram E. Left Tan. Bangaram S. 73° E. Centre of Agathi S. 29° W. in 5½ fathoms.
Bitra	East extremity of island N. 25° W. about ½ M. Distant in 11 fathoms.
Chetlat	Left Tan. N. 53° W. South end of Centre part of reef S. 76° E. Right Tan. S. 37° E. in 4 fathoms.
Kadamath	Left Tan. Kadamath N. 45½° E. Right Tan. Kadamath S. 7° E. Left Tan. Ameni S. 15½° W. in 4 fathoms.
Kalpeni	Mosque No. 7° E. at 3 cables. in 6½ fathoms.
Kavarathi	South Tan. N. 87° E at 4½ cables in 4 fathoms.
Kilten	N.W. Point bearing ½° S. 79½° E. at 2·2 Cables in 3¾ fathoms.
Minicoy	Smallpox island. S. 5° E. Light-house. S. 25° E. Beacon on reef. S. 69° E. } (T)
Suheli	South island S. 24° W. Right Tan. of North island S. 4° W. Left Tan. of North island S. 13° E. in 5¾ fathoms.

APPENDIX VI.

REGULATION No. I OF 1912.

[THE LACCADIVE ISLANDS AND MINICOY REGULATION, 1912.]

[*Received the assent of the Governor-General on the 22nd January 1912; published in the* Gazette of India *on the 3rd February 1912 and in the* Fort Saint George Gazette *Extraordinary on the 1st idem.*]

A Regulation to declare the Law applicable to the Laccadive Islands and Minicoy.

WHEREAS it is expedient to declare the law applicable to the Laccadive Islands and Minicoy; It is hereby enacted as follows:—

CHAPTER I.

PRELIMINARY.

Short title and extent.

1. (*1*) This Regulation may be called the Laccadive Islands and Minicoy Regulation, 1912; and

(*2*) It extends to the Laccadive Islands and Minicoy.

Definitions.

2. In this Regulation, unless there is anything repugnant in the subject or context,—

(i) "the islands" mean the Laccadive Islands and Minicoy:

(ii) "the Inspecting officer" means any officer directed by the Local Government or Collector to inspect the islands or any of them: and

XLV of 1860.

(iii) words and expressions used herein and defined in the Indian Penal Code[1] have the same meaning respectively attributed to them in that Code.

CHAPTER II.

LAW APPLICABLE.

Law applicable.

II of 1819. III of 1858. XIV of 1874.

3. Notwithstanding anything in any enactment now in force, this Regulation, the [2]Madras State Prisoners Regulation, 1819, the [3]State Prisoners Act, 1858, and the [4]Scheduled Districts Act, 1874, shall be the only enactments in force in the islands.

---

[1] General Acts, Vol. I.

[2] *Supra.*

[3] General Acts, Vol. I.

[4] General Acts, Vol. II.

CHAPTER III.

CRIMINAL JUSTICE.

Offences triable by inspecting officer or Collector.

4. (*1*) Whoever commits any of the following offences shall be liable to the punishment mentioned below in respect of such offence :—

Offence	Punishment
Rioting	Imprisonment which may extend to two years, or fine, or both.
Giving false evidence	Imprisonment which may extend to seven years, and fine.
Murder	Death or transportation for life.
Culpable homicide not amounting to murder.	Transportation for life or imprisonment which may extend to ten years.
Causing death by rash or negligent act.	Imprisonment which may extend to two years, or fine.
Grievous hurt	Imprisonment which may extend to seven years, and fine.
Wrongful confinement	Imprisonment which may extend to one year, or fine.
Kidnapping	Imprisonment which may extend to seven years, and fine.
Rape	Transportation for life or imprisonment which may extend to ten years, and fine.
Extortion	Imprisonment which may extend to three years, or fine, or both.
Robbery	Rigorous imprisonment which may extend to ten years, and fine.
Dacoity	Transportation for life, or rigorous imprisonment which may extend to ten years, and fine.
Criminal misappropriation ...	Imprisonment which may extend to two years, or fine, or both.
Criminal breach of trust	Imprisonment which may extend to three years, or fine, or both.
Dishonestly receiving stolen property.	Imprisonment which may extend to three years, or fine, or both.
Cheating	Imprisonment which may extend to one year, or fine, or both.
Mischief by fire	Imprisonment which may extend to seven years, and fine.
Forgery	Imprisonment which may extend to two years, or fine.

(*2*) When any offence specified in sub-section (*1*) has been committed, the local amin shall hold an investigation, and, if a *prima facie* case is made out against any person, such person shall be charged before and tried by the Inspecting officer or the Collector or any of the Collector's assistants empowered by him by general or special order in this behalf.

(*3*) The Inspecting officer or the Collector or any assistant of the Collector empowered under sub-section (*2*), when trying a case in accordance with sub-section (*2*), shall, when the trial is held in the islands, sit with two or more island assessors.

Minor offences and punishment.

5. Whoever—

(*a*) commits any of the following offences, namely :—
theft, criminal force, assault, hurt, criminal trespass,

(*b*) uses abusive language to another,

(*c*) obstructs any person in seizing stray cattle,

(*d*) without reasonable cause fails to attend the kachahri when ordered to do so;

(e) causes mischief to property otherwise than by fire,

(f) makes any imputation concerning any person knowing that such imputation is liable to harm the reputation of the person,

(g) being convicted or charged with an offence and being in lawful custody escapes from such custody,

conviction by the amin shall be punishable with imprisonment for a erm which may extend to fifteen days, or with fine which may extend to fifteen rupees, or with both.

6. Subject to the control of the Governor-General in Council, the Governor in Council may, by notification in the Fort St. George Gazette, add to the list of offences specified in section 4, sub-section (1), and section 5, and prescribe the punishments for the offences so added. Addition to list of offences.

7. Whoever fails to give information of a birth or death in his house hall be punishable with fine which may extend to five rupees. Failure to give information of birth or death.

8. (1) Whoever, when ordered to do so by the amin,— Failure to obey reasonable order of amin.

(a) fails to assist in launching or drawing up a boat,

(b) fails to attend when called upon to assist in protecting coconut plantations from the ravages of rats,

all be punishable with fine which may extend to two rupees:

Provided that a fine imposed under clause (b) may be refunded if the offender within forty-eight hours makes reparation to the satisfaction of the amin and assessors.

(2) Whoever, in a case not provided for by sub-section (1), disobeys any reasonable order of an amin or other public servant, shall be punishable with imprisonment which may extend to fifteen days, or fine which may extend to fifteen rupees, or with both.

9. (1) The local amin of each island shall have jurisdiction to try persons accused of offences specified in sections 5 to 8 in the island and inflict on persons found guilty of any such offence the punishment prescribed therefor. Jurisdiction and constitution of the Court of the amin.

(2) The local amin in the exercise of such jurisdiction shall sit with four or more assessors called karnavars in the islands. Such assessors shall be specially appointed by the Collector or Inspecting officer for life, subject to good behaviour.

(3) Whenever an amin is of opinion that an accused person tried before him is guilty of an offence specified in section 5 or in section 8, sub-section (2), and ought to receive a more severe punishment than he is empowered to inflict, he shall submit his proceedings, and forward the accused, to the Inspecting officer or the Collector, and such officer may pass such order as he thinks fit: Provided that he shall not pass any sentence of imprisonment exceeding one year.

10. (1) The amin may take cognizance of cases on complaint or on his own initiative. Procedure of amin in criminal cases.

(2) In every case the amin shall make a memorandum of the evidence of the prosecution witnesses, the plea of the accused, and the evidence of the defence witnesses,

(3) The evidence shall be taken in the presence of the accused, and the accused and the complainant shall be allowed to cross-examine the witnesses for the other side.

(4) The amin shall deliver a written judgment, recording therein the opinions of the assessors sitting with him and the reasons for his own decision.

Withdrawal or transfer by Collector.

11. (1) The Collector may withdraw to his own file any case pending before the Inspecting officer or an amin.

(2) The Collector may transfer any case pending before himself or before the Inspecting officer to any of his Divisional officers for trial.

(3) The Inspecting officer may withdraw to his own file any case pending before an amin.

Appeals from decisions of amin.

12. From any sentence or order passed by an amin an appeal shall lie either to the Collector or the Inspecting officer in cases in which the Collector or the Inspecting officer grants special leave to appeal.

Appeals from decision of the Island. Inspecting officer or Divisional officer.

13. Any person convicted by the Inspecting officer or by a Divisional officer may appeal (a) to the High Court if the sentence is one of death or of imprisonment for five years or upwards, and (b) to the Collector in other cases if the sentence exceeds three months' imprisonment or one hundred rupees fine.

Appeals from the Collector.

14. From any sentence or order passed by the Collector as a Court of original criminal jurisdiction an appeal shall lie to the High Court.

No second appeals.

15. No second appeal shall lie in any case whatever.

Provision as to stamps.

16. Every appeal shall be stamped with an eight-anna stamp, and shall be accompanied by a copy on stamped copy paper of the judgment or order appealed against:

Provided that nothing in this section shall apply to an appeal by a prisoner.

Limitation of appeal.

17. Every appeal shall be filed within six months from the date of the judgment or order appealed against:

Provided that the months of June, July, August and September shall be excluded in reckoning such period.

Representation of parties.

18. No pleader shall be allowed in any Court except with the special permission of the Collector. Parties may, however, be represented by their island mukhtyars.

Powers-of-attorney.

19. Every mukhtyar, appearing before a Court on the mainland on behalf of a party in the islands, must produce a stamped mukhtyarnama or power-of-attorney bearing a court-fee stamp of eight annas.

Detention of convicts in common jail in certain cases.

20. Any person convicted of a criminal offence and sentenced to a term of imprisonment exceeding two months by a Court on the islands, or to any term of imprisonment by a Court on the mainland, may be sent for imprisonment to the Cannanore Central Jail.

CHAPTER IV.

CIVIL JUSTICE.

21. All questions relating to any rights claimed or set up in the Civil Courts of the islands shall be determined in accordance with any custom not manifestly unjust or immoral governing the parties or property concerned, and, in the absence of any such custom, according to justice, equity and good conscience. Law to be administered in Civil Courts.

22. The local amin of each island sitting with four or more assessors shall be the Civil Court for the island, and shall have jurisdiction over all civil claims arising therein. Constitution of Civil Courts.

23. Every suit shall be commenced by presenting a plaint to the amin having jurisdiction over the suit. Commencement of suit.

24. The Collector or the Inspecting officer may transfer any civil suit to his own file and shall then proceed to try it sitting with two or more of the island assessors. The Collector may transfer any such suit from his own file to that of any of his Divisional officers, who shall proceed to try the case with two or more such assessors. Transferred suits.

25. (*1*) The Collector or the Inspecting officer may refer any case for disposal or report to two or more of the island assessors. When it is referred for disposal, the assessors shall report their decision to the Court referring the case. Reference to assessors.

(*2*) The parties may challenge any assessor, and on sufficient reason being given another assessor shall be selected in his place.

(*3*) The parties shall be allowed to attend the hearing of the suit in person or by a mukhtyar, and the evidence shall be taken in open Court.

(*4*) The officer trying the suit shall make a memorandum of the evidence of each witness as it is given, and shall, after the conclusion of the hearing, pronounce judgment in open Court either in the presence of the parties or after notice to them. The judgment shall be in writing and shall contain the points for determination and the decision thereon.

26. (*1*) An appeal shall lie from the decision of the amin to the Inspecting officer or to the Collector. The Collector may transfer any such appeal to the Inspecting officer or any other of his Divisional officers for disposal. Appeals.

(*2*) No appeal shall ordinarily lie from a decision of the Inspecting officer in the exercise of his original jurisdiction, but an appeal may be admitted by the Collector if sufficient grounds are shown. From a decision of a Divisional officer in the exercise of his original jurisdiction an appeal shall lie to the Collector.

(*3*) Save as otherwise provided in section 31, an appeal shall lie to the High Court from any decision of the Collector in the exercise of his original jurisdiction.

27. The provisions of sections 15, 16, 17, 18 and 19 shall also apply to civil cases. Application of certain sections to civil cases.

28. All decrees shall ordinarily be executed by the amin of the island where the suit was instituted. But the Collector or the Inspecting officer may execute his own decrees if convenient. Execution of decrees.

Resistance to execution.

29. If a judgment-debtor wilfully refuses to obey the decree of the Court, he shall be liable to punishment under section 8, sub-section (*2*), and where the amin is of opinion that such punishment is inadequate, the procedure prescribed in section 9, sub-section (*3*), shall be followed.

Attachment and sale.

30. Cases in which attachment and sale of property is found necessary shall be reserved for the Inspecting officer, who shall attach the property of the judgment-debtor and sell it in execution of the decree.

Service of process.

31. Decrees or processes issued by a mainland Court against an islander, or by one island Court against a person residing in another island, shall be forwarded to the Collector for execution and he shall cause it to be executed unless for reasons to be recorded in writing he may consider execution inadvisable, in which case he may refuse to execute it. In the case of any such refusal an appeal shall lie to the Governor in Council.

Saving of inherent power of Civil Court.

32. Nothing in this Regulation shall be deemed to limit or otherwise affect the inherent power of a Civil Court to make such orders as may be necessary for the ends of justice or to prevent abuse of the powers of the Court.

CHAPTER V.

Miscellaneous.

Power of Governor in Council to exclude inhabitants of mainland from islands.

33. The Governor in Council may by order prohibit persons residing on the mainland from visiting or taking up their residence in the islands, and may require persons ordinarily residing on the mainland who have taken up their residence in the islands to leave the islands; and he may make such rules as he deems fit in pursuance of the above.

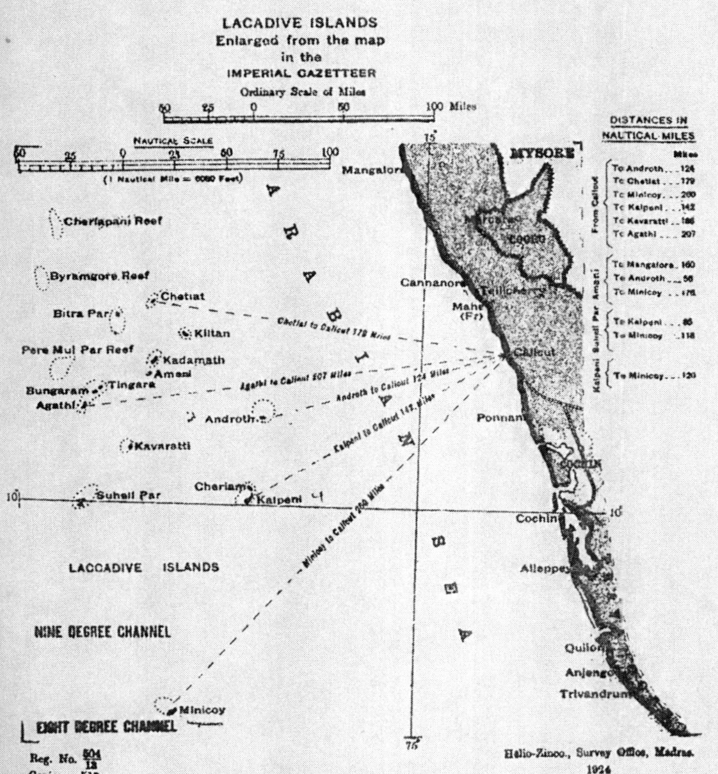
LACADIVE ISLANDS
Enlarged from the map
in the
IMPERIAL GAZETTEER
Ordinary Scale of Miles
50 25 0 50 100 Miles
NAUTICAL SCALE
50 25 0 25 50 75 100
(1 Nautical Mile = 6080 Feet)
DISTANCES IN NAUTICAL MILES
Miles
From Calicut
To Androth ... 124
To Chetlat ... 179
To Minicoy ... 200
To Kalpeni ... 142
To Kavaratti ... 186
To Agathi ... 207
Amini
To Mangalore .. 160
To Androth ... 56
To Minicoy ... 176
Suheli Par
To Kalpeni ... 86
To Minicoy ... 118
Kalpeni
To Minicoy ... 120
MYSORE
COORG
Mangalore
Cannanore
Tellicherry
Mahe (Fr)
Calicut
Ponnani
COCHIN
Cochin
Alleppey
Quilon
Anjengo
Trivandrum
Cherlapani Reef
Byramgore Reef
Chetlat
Bitra Par
Kiltan
Pere Mul Par Reef
Kadamath
Amini
Bungaram
Tingara
Agathi
Androth
Kavaratti
Cheriam
Kalpeni
Suheli Par
Minicoy
Chetlat to Calicut 179 Miles
Agathi to Calicut 207 Miles
Androth to Calicut 124 Miles
Kalpeni to Calicut 142 Miles
Minicoy to Calicut 200 Miles
LACCADIVE ISLANDS
NINE DEGREE CHANNEL
EIGHT DEGREE CHANNEL
Reg. No. 504/12
Copies 512
Helio-Zinco., Survey Office, Madras.
1924

INDEX.